TRACTATUS FIGURARUM

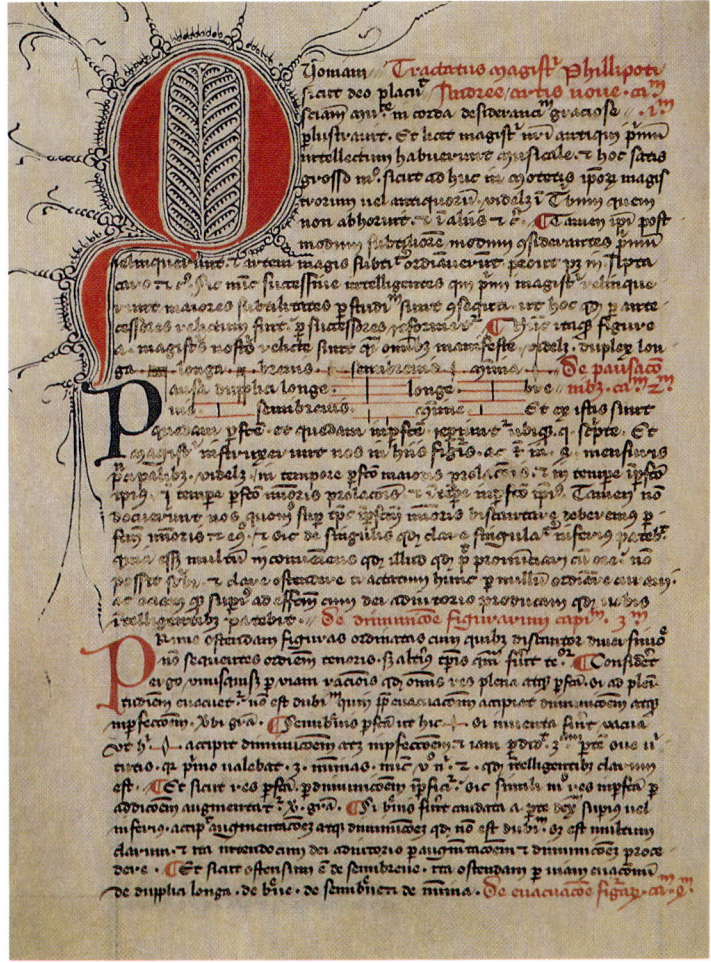

Chicago, Newberry Library, Ms. 54.1, f. 7v
(Courtesy of The Newberry Library, Chicago)

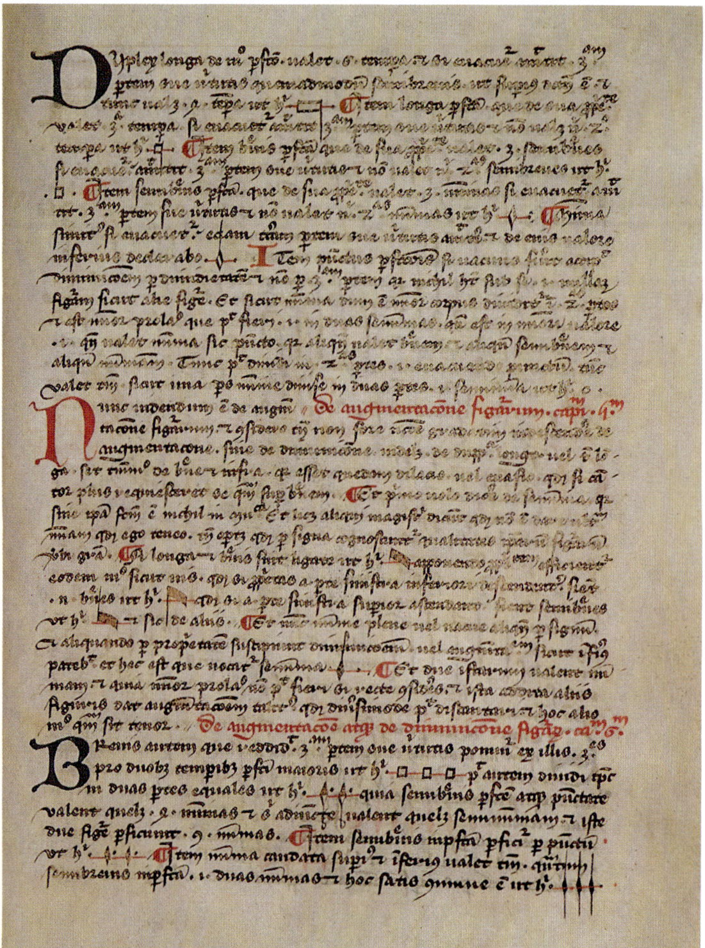

Chicago, Newberry Library, Ms. 54.1, f. 8r
(Courtesy of The Newberry Library, Chicago)

Chicago, Newberry Library, Ms. 54.1, f. 8v
(Courtesy of The Newberry Library, Chicago)

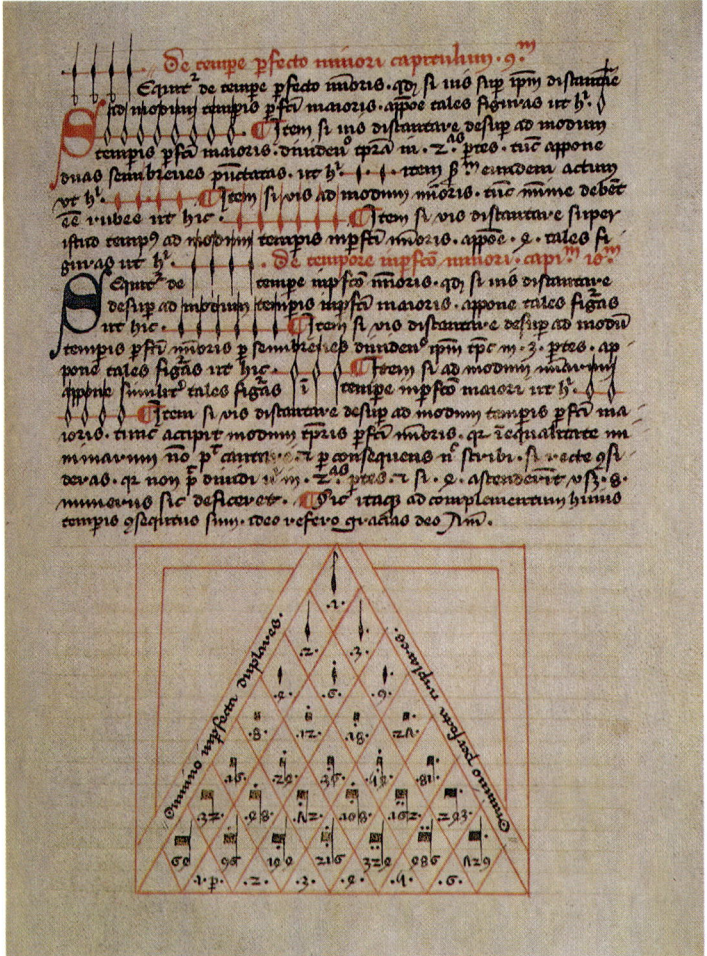

Chicago, Newberry Library, Ms. 54.1, f. 9r
(Courtesy of The Newberry Library, Chicago)

Tractatus Figurarum

Notational complexity, or *subtilitas*, was engendered in the late fourteenth century by a thorough probing of all the rhythmic possibilities within the accepted mensurations. As French and Italian notational practices began to diverge at the beginning of the *Ars nova*, composers invented new rhythmic symbols—*figurae*—as their innovations required, and this resulted in a variety of notations that were as confusing to the musician of that day as they are to the modern scholar.

In the third quarter of the fourteenth century, a notational system combining elements of the French and Italian systems was put forth in the *Tractatus figurarum*. This system proposed a standard set of *figurae* for simultaneous combinations of any two of the four prolations of the French mensural system.

Coussemaker's 1869 edition of the *Tractatus figurarum*, which attributes the treatise to Philippus de Caserta, was based on his knowledge of only four of the fourteen surviving manuscripts. A critical study of all the sources, including the important Newberry Library manuscript, leads to a corrected version of the text and allows the entire system to be resurrected. The critical edition is joined with a fully annotated translation on facing pages. An Introduction discusses the authorship and theory of the treatise, as well as placing it within the context of the music theory of the fourteenth century. Full descriptions of all the manuscript sources and four full-color plates of the Newberry Library manuscript are included.

The system of the *Tractatus figurarum* was beautifully creative, but it did not meet with success. Nevertheless, the treatise proves itself invaluable to the study of the *Ars subtilior* in revealing certain basic notational principles that may be applied to surviving musical compositions, illuminating the notational subtleties in which this music delighted.

Philip E. Schreur is the Music Librarian at the University of California, Davis.

Greek and Latin Music Theory

Thomas J. Mathiesen,
General Editor
Indiana University

Jon Solomon,
Associate Editor
University of Arizona

Previously published in this series

Prosdocimo de' Beldomandi, *Contrapunctus*
edited and translated by Jan Herlinger

The Berkeley Manuscript, University of California
Music Library, MS. 744 (*olim* Phillipps 4450)
edited and translated by Oliver B. Ellsworth

Sextus Empiricus, ΠΡΟΣ ΜΟΥΣΙΚΟΥΣ,
Against the Musicians (Adversus musicos)
edited and translated by Denise Davidson Greaves

Prosdocimo de' Beldomandi, *Brevis summula
proportionum quantum ad musicam pertinet*
and *Parvus tractatulus de modo
monacordum dividendi*
edited and translated by Jan Herlinger

Gaspar Stoquerus, *De musica verbali*
edited and translated by Albert C. Rotola, S.J.

TRACTATUS FIGURARUM

Treatise on Noteshapes

A new critical text and
translation on facing pages,
with an introduction, annotations,
and *indices verborum*
and *nominum et rerum* by

Philip E. Schreur

University of Nebraska Press
Lincoln and London

Copyright © 1989 by the
University of Nebraska Press
All rights reserved
Manufactured in the United States of America

The paper in this book meets the minimum
requirements of American National Standard
for Information Sciences—Permanence of
Paper for Printed Library Materials,
ANSI Z39.48.-1984.

Library of Congress Cataloging-in-Publication Data
Tractatus figurarum. English & Latin.
Tractatus figurarum = Treatise on noteshapes.
(Greek and Latin music theory)
Includes bibliographical references.
1. Musical notation—Early works to 1800.
2. Music—Theory—500–1400—Early works to 1800.
I. Schreur, Philip Evan. II. Title. III. Title:
Treatise on noteshapes. IV. Series.
MT5.5.T713   1990   780'.148   89–22569
ISBN 0-8032-4203-4

CONTENTS

FRONTISPIECE: Chicago, Newberry Library, Ms. 54.1, ff. 7v–9r i

PREFACE xi

INTRODUCTION 1

    Authorship 3
    The Evolution of the *Tractatus*'s Notation 9
    The Theory of the *Tractatus* 11
    The *Figurae* 15
    The Epilogue 20
    The Manuscripts 25
    The Stemma 59
    The Edition 63

CONSPECTUS CODICUM ET NOTARUM 65

TRACTATUS FIGURARUM 66

    Prologus 66
    Capitulum primum 68
    Capitulum secundum 70
    Capitulum tertium 72
    Capitulum quartum 76
    Capitulum quintum 80
    Capitulum sextum 82
    Capitulum septimum 88
    Capitulum octavum 92
    Capitulum nonum 94
    Capitulum decimum 96
    Epilogus 98

APPENDIX 105

INDEX VERBORUM 115

INDEX NOMINUM ET RERUM 121

PREFACE

Notational complexity, or *subtilitas*, was engendered in the late fourteenth century by a thorough probing of all rhythmic possibilities within the accepted mensurations. As French and Italian notational practices began to diverge at the beginning of the *Ars nova*, composers invented new rhythmic symbols—*figurae*—as their innovations required, and this resulted in a variety of notations that were as confusing to the musician of that day as they are to the modern scholar.

In the third quarter of the fourteenth century, a notational system combining elements of the French and Italian systems was put forth in the *Tractatus figurarum*. This system proposed a standard set of *figurae* for simultaneous combinations of any two of the four prolations of the French mensural system.

Coussemaker's 1869 edition of the *Tractatus figurarum*, which attributes the treatise to Philippus de Caserta, was based on his knowledge of only four of the surviving manuscripts. A critical study of all the sources, including the important Newberry Library manuscript, leads to a corrected version of the text and allows the entire system to be resurrected. The edition includes an Epilogue to the *Tractatus figurarum* that discusses the concept of *traynour*—a term used to identify an intensified level of rhythmic activity first mentioned in the *Quatuor principalia musicae*. An extensive set of examples of *traynour* following the *Tractatus figurarum* in the Seville manuscript is included in an Appendix.

First and foremost, I should like to thank Professor Thomas J. Mathiesen for his unstinting aid in the revision of the *Tractatus figurarum*, without which this edition would not have been possible. Thanks are also due to the staff of the Music Library of Stanford University for the gracious access provided to its microfilm collection during the final stages of revision.

Work for this edition was funded in part by a fellowship from The Newberry Library, Chicago, and the University of California Research Grants for Librarians (Librarians Association of the University of California, Davis). Permission to reproduce the manuscript pages was given courtesy of The Newberry Library. I should also like to thank the Division of Research and Graduate Development of Indiana University for generous grants in support of the series Greek and Latin Music Theory.

To all those involved in this project from its roots in my fascination with the *ars subtilior* to the publication of the *Tractatus figurarum* in this series, I give my heartfelt thanks. Unreserved support was given at every juncture and is a debt I can never repay.

INTRODUCTION

Subtlety and intentional obscurity, while having a similar effect in the eyes of the uninitiated observer, are diametrically opposed in intent, for there is a yawning chasm between the subtlety of making fine distinctions and the willful obscuring of interrelationships. The fourteenth century was an era of many fine distinctions. Scholasticism had reached its zenith, and this unification of language, ideas, and terminology brought about by a common university education allowed a shared rigor to be applied to all seven of the liberal arts. Detailed inquiries through the art of logic into the perception of universals, or *intentio secunda*,[1] were matched by increasing sophistication in the definition of musical concepts through the universal principles of mathematics. According to Thomas Aquinas, "Logicus et mathematicus considerant tantum res secundum principia formalia."[2] Moreover, it was these principles elucidated by such mathematicians as Johannes de Muris in his *Notitia artis musicae*[3] and their development by innovative composers of the fourteenth century that led to the *ars subtilior*—the more subtle art.

The *ars subtilior* has long been viewed as a misshapen flower blooming from the muddied and decaying quagmire of Medieval thought before the refreshing and renewing vigor of the Renaissance. The music has been called

---

[1] Anton Dumitriu, *History of Logic*, 4 vols. (Tunbridge Wells, Kent: Abacus Press, 1977), 2:53–54.

[2] "The logician and the mathematician view things only acording to their formal principles" (St. Thomas Aquinas, "De potentia," ed. R. P. Pauli [and] M. Pession, in *Questiones disputatae*, 2 vols., 8th ed. by P. Bazzi [Taurini: Marietti, 1949], 2:160b; quoted in ibid., 2:59–60).

[3] *Johannis de Muris Notitia artis musicae et compendium musicae practicae, Petrus* [sic] *de Sancto Dionysio Tractatus de musica,* ed. Ulrich Michels, Corpus scriptorum de musica, no. 17 (n.p.: American Institute of Musicology, 1972).

inconsistent and willfully complex,[4] but on the contrary, nothing could be further from the truth. It was born of a time alive with the vigorous exploration of rhythmic and harmonic possibilities based on reasoned extensions of traditional mathematical and musical principles. We must also acknowledge the fact that this music was both performed and enjoyed, thus being careful not to attribute our notational confusion to an era that depended upon crystalline distinctions.

There are, however, factors contributing to today's confusion—factors not of our own making. First, there are copyists' errors in the few remaining musical sources, a problem that plagues any manuscript tradition. Second, there is the divergence between French and Italian notational practices that continued to grow throughout the *ars nova*. By the end of the fourteenth century, however, these two disparate national styles merged under French cultural domination, and a new tradition developed incorporating elements of both.[5] This new tradition was not uniform, varying in its proportion of French and Italian elements by time, place, and even composer. Last, rhythmic exploration (and hence notation) was undergoing a tremendous development. The *ars nova* was a revolution in notation in which composers and performers were freed from the strictures of modal patterns imposed by neumatic groupings and dots of division. With the development of differentiated noteshapes for specified temporal durations, composers were free to divide the basic brevis unit as they pleased, a development that culminated in the *ars subtilior*. These composers, then, would often have to invent a new *figura*, that is to say, a new noteshape for a particular rhythm they wished to express because it had never before been written. Although this fantastic explosion of new *figurae* provides much of today's confusion over the *ars subtilior,* they were based upon notational principles in which the composers had been trained, and at least in the case of the composer Senleches, once developed, they would be used consistently throughout his compositions. In determining the probable duration of any new *figurae* in one of these compositions, we must be aware of a composer's national background or training, his other compositions, and most important, the theoretical principles with which he was working.

As musical taste shifted in the early fifteenth century, the stunning rhythmic advances of the *ars subtilior* were abandoned before a theorist such as

---

[4]Willi Apel, *The Notation of Polyphonic Music: 900–1600,* 5th ed. (Cambridge, Massachusetts: The Mediaeval Academy of America, 1953), p. 403.

[5]Ibid., p. 385.

Johannes de Muris or a music historian such as Jacques de Liège could document its development. What do survive, though, are a few practical guides on the performance of the then current notation, much as Philippe de Vitry's *Ars nova* is a performer's guide to the notational features of the period that is named for it. One such guide is the *Tractatus figurarum*, and just as the *Ars nova* boldly proclaims the fundamentals of the new art, so the *Tractatus figurarum* lays bare the framework of the more subtle art.

The only modern edition of this treatise exists in Edmond de Coussemaker's *Scriptores*,[6] in which it has been attributed to Philippus de Caserta. This version was unfortunately based upon a few corrupt sources and in this form is illogical and inconsistent. In establishing a new critical edition, it was necessary to study all fourteen of the surviving sources and through the careful collation of both text and notation, establish a reliable version of the author's text.

While it is true the system proposed in the *Tractatus figurarum* was never accepted into the mainstream of fourteenth-century theory or composition, as is shown from its lack of use in any surviving music, its interest to musicians of the time is clear from the number of surviving copies. The principles used in its creation also reveal much about the theory of notation at the end of the fourteenth century.

Authorship

Authorship is the first question raised when examining the *Tractatus figurarum*. The treatise has been attributed to Philippus de Caserta on the authority of Coussemaker,[7] but only one source, the Faenza Codex,[8] attributes the *Tractatus figurarum* to him, and it was on this single source that Coussemaker based his attribution. On the other hand, four of the sources[9] attribute the *Tractatus* to Egidius de Murino and link it to his *De modo componendi*.

---

[6]*Scriptorum de musica medii aevi nova series a Gerbertina altera* (henceforward: CS), 4 vols., ed. Edmond de Coussemaker (Paris: Durand, 1864–76; reprint ed., Hildesheim: Olms, 1963), 3:118–24.

[7]Ibid.

[8]Faenza, Biblioteca Comunale, Ms. 117 (henceforward: Fa), ff. 15v–17r.

[9]London, British Library, Additional 4909 (henceforward: Lo), ff. 11v–14v; Roma, Biblioteca Apostolica Vaticana, lat. 5321 (henceforward: Ro5), ff. 6r–7v; Siena, Biblioteca Comunale, L.V.30 (henceforward: Si), ff. 41r–44r; and Washington, Library of Congress, ML171.J6 (henceforward: Wa), ff. 70v–74r.

Finally, the earliest datable source[10] gives the author as Phillipoctus Andrea, a name otherwise unknown. In the remaining eight manuscripts, the *Tractatus figurarum* is recorded without author attribution. By a careful examination of the *Tractatus* itself, and the few auxiliary sources still available, some degree of clarity can be brought to this muddied question.

Since the publication of Coussemaker's *Scriptores*, the treatise has been ascribed to Philippus de Caserta. In his article "Der Tractatus Figurarum,"[11] Wulf Arlt provides a summary of the evidence for and against the authors variously attested and in so doing offers more support for Philippus de Caserta than merely the attribution of the Faenza Codex. The copies of the theoretical sources contained in the Faenza Codex were a product of Frater Bonadies, a student of Hothby and teacher of Gaffurius.[12] His preoccupation with music theory is attested by the variety of theoretical sources copied, but his attribution to Philippus de Caserta is corroborated by no other source. There is, however, a commentary on the *Tractatus figurarum* preserved in the same Seville manuscript that contains three copies of the treatise itself,[13] and in this commentary the *Tractatus* is ascribed to Philippus de Caserta:

> Secundum magistrum Philippotum de Caserta dicta tempora possunt augmentare per alias diversas figuras, sicut inferius apparent.[14]

The attribution in this source cannot be taken lightly, for the noteshapes that follow are extremely accurate—more so, in fact, than many of the *Tractatus* sources and so perhaps derive from an early, carefully copied source.

---

[10]Chicago, Newberry Library, Ms. 54.1 (henceforward: Ch), ff. 7v–9r.

[11]Wulf Arlt, "Der Tractatus figurarum—ein Beitrag zur Musiklehre der 'Ars subtilior,'" *Schweizer Beiträge zur Musikwissenschaft* 1 (1972): 35–53.

[12]Albert Seay, "Hothby, John," *New Grove Dictionary of Music and Musicians* 8 (1980): 729.

[13]Sevilla, Catedral Metropolitana, Biblioteca Capitular y Colombina, 5.2.25 (henceforward: Se), ff. 93r–94r. The three sources for the *Tractatus figurarum* are found on ff. 84r–85v, f. 87r, and ff. 114r–116r (henceforward: Se1, Se2, and Se3 respectively).

[14]"According to Master Philippus de Caserta, the tempora spoken of can be augmented through other diverse noteshapes, as are shown below" (*Mensurabilis musicae tractatuli,* vol. 1, ed. F. Alberto Gallo, Antiquae musicae italicae scriptores, no. 1 [Bologna: Università degli Studi di Bologna, 1966], p. 81).

The most damaging evidence against the authorship of Philippus de Caserta is brought by his own works. It is not unreasonable to assume that a composer so interested in noteshapes would use these noteshapes in his own compositions. Nevertheless, none of the noteshapes proposed in the *Tractatus figurarum* appears in any of Philippus's compositions. The examples shown below are taken from his Ballade *En remirant,* which occurs in both the Chantilly and Modena codices. In both sources, the same noteshapes are given for these complex rhythms, noteshapes different from those in the *Tractatus figurarum.*

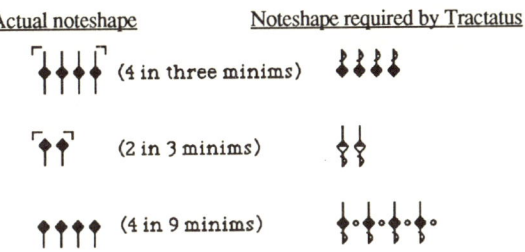

This evidence against the authorship of Philippus de Caserta is not conclusive, however, for music by him may yet be discovered that makes use of the noteshapes from the *Tractatus figurarum.*

The ascription to Egidius de Murino is as elusive a claim to prove or disprove as that to Philippus. Although it is true that four sources ascribe the *Tractatus figurarum* to Egidius, Arlt rightly points out that all four derive from the same progenitor and so only one source had the original ascription.[15] In this case, the single attribution to Egidius ostensibly carries only as much weight as that of Bonadies to Philippus. There is, however, a reference to Egidius contained in a fifteenth-century source. Ramos de Pareja, in his

---

[15]Arlt, p. 44.

Musica pratica, quotes from the *Tractatus* and attributes it to Egidius.[16] From Ramos's quotations, it is clear he was working with a source from the A group in the stemma,[17] the same group that attributes the *Tractatus* to Egidius. Thus, Ramos's authority can be traced to the same progenitor as those above.

It has been argued, moreover, that the attribution to Egidius in these sources was made in error by a copyist who mistakenly joined the *Tractatus figurarum* to the *De modo componendi*, which is truly by Egidius.[18] The copyist was perhaps fooled by both authors' fascination with the concept of *subtilitas*[19] into not only attributing each treatise to the same author but also

---

[16]"Egidius vero de morino dicit quod ideo dicitur prolatio quia tempus dividit in partes minutiores ut melius proferatur. Nam absurdum esset ut ait quod potest pronunciari non possit scribi (Tertia pars, Tractatus primus, Capitulum primum). Egidius de marino de minima tractans ait merito tertiam debet amittere partem. Punctus vero quia nihil habet sub se tantum medietatem (Tertia pars, Tractatus primus, Capitulum tertium). Ponebant etiam albas id est in medio vacuas ut nos facimus modo quando sed in prup (?) tu rubeum colorem ut placet egidio de marino non habebant (Tertia pars, Tractatus primus, Capitulum tertium) (Bartolomeus Ramos de Pareja, *Musica pratica* [Bologna: Baltasar de Hiriberia, 1482; reprint ed., Bologna: Forni, n.d.]) (Egidius de morino says that it is called prolatio because the tempus is divided into smaller parts so that it can be better performed. For it would be absurd, as he says, that [what] could be sung could not be written [3rd part, 1st treatise, chap. 1] Egidius de marino, in treating the minima, says that, by merit, it should lose a third part, while a dot, because there is nothing below it, [should lose] only a half [3rd part, 1st treatise, chap. 3]. Also, they were using white [notes] (that is, hollow in the middle), as in the way we do, but when [?] they do not have red color, as is pleasing to Egidius de marino [3rd part, 1st treatise, chap. 3])."

[17]The phrase "nam esset absurdum ..." is found in Wa and a variant of it in Si (see notes to 72.1). Likewise, the word "medietatem" in conjunction with the hollow dot occurs in Ro5 (see notes to 78.2). Since both these variants do not occur in the same source, Ramos must have been familiar with the hypothetical source γ from which this group derives. See pp. 59–61.

[18]Arlt, p. 45.

[19]"Item potes ibi adjungere aliam subtilitatem, et hoc est, si vis, potes eam facere de modo perfecto ... (CS, 3:125a). Sciendum est quod per tenores supradictos potest inveniri quamplures alii modi et deduci alii tenores per viam subtilitatis, et ideo non est necesse contratenores componere. Plures eorum qui possunt inveniri, quando esistit subtilis cantor, potest facere alios tenores quamplures eorum ... (CS, 3:127b). Si majores subtilitates cupis habere quam in isto volumine continentur, tunc stude fortior in musicam ... (CS, 3:128a). (There you can impart another subtlety, and that is, if you wish, you can use perfect modus .... It must be known that, through the

conjoining them through continuous chapter numeration.[20] *De modo componendi,* however, is concerned with a much simpler style of composition more reminiscent of the beginning of the century than the end, and it is difficult to believe that both are by the same person.[21]

A further indication arguing against Egidius de Murino's authorship is given by his name: it is improbable that the author of the *Tractatus figurarum* should be French.[22] The first clue pointing towards Italian authorship is given in chapter 2 (70.6[23]), where the author lists the "quatuor mensurae principales," or four principal mensurations. When discussing mensural theory, French theorists typically spoke of only four mensurations; it was the Italian theorists who spoke of more.

A stronger indication, however, is given by the importance placed on the semiminima.

> Et primo volo dicere de semiminima quia sine ipsa factum est nichil in musica (80.7–8)[24]

---

aforesaid tenors, there can be discovered many more of another type, and other tenors can be deduced through the path of subtlety, and thus it is not necessary to compose contratenors. The many of them which can be discovered, when the cantor would be subtle, can make many other tenors of them .... If you desire to have more subtlety than is contained in this volume, then study music more diligently)."

[20]All four sources of the *Tractatus* in the A group (Lo, Ro5, Si, Wa) are followed by *De modo componendi* without pause, and in the case of Ro5 and Wa, *De modo* is numbered as chapter 4 of the *Tractatus figurarum.*

[21]Arlt, p. 45.

[22]In his article on Egidius de Murino for the *New Grove Dictionary of Music and Musicians,* Gilbert Reaney summarizes the evidence on Egidius's person and identifies the place name Morino or Murino as referring to the diocese of La Thérouanne in Northern France.

[23]The page and line numbers refer to the present edition.

[24]"And first, I wish to speak of the semiminima because no music is made without it."

> Et ista [semiminima] adjuncta aliis figuris dat augmentationem taliter quod diversimode potest discantari et hoc alio modo quam sit tenor (82.5–7)[25]

It is unlikely that someone trained in French theory would base his system of notation upon a note whose very existence was theoretically uncertain. Yet, it would not be unreasonable for an Italian trained in the now predominant French style and immersed in his tradition rich in semiminimae to have done so.

The semiminima is first mentioned in Philippe de Vitry's *Ars nova* written in the early 1320s.[26] Already at the point of its invention, its very existence is questioned, for in chapter 15 de Vitry states that one may rename the semiminima and the minima, calling the semiminima a minima and the minima semiminor, thus eliminating semiminima from accepted note names.[27] It is not surprising that the reactionary Jacques de Liège condemns the semiminima along with all the other supposed advances of the new art,[28] but even one of the most honored moderns, Johannes de Muris, does not include the semiminima in his list of acceptable noteshapes.[29] As late as the 1350s, this note

---

[25]"And this [semiminima] added to other noteshapes gives augmentation in such a way that it can be discanted in various manners and another mode than the tenor would be."

[26]"That which is worth two minimae is called minor, as was said earlier; [that] which [is worth] one is named minima; [that] which [is worth] half of a minima is named semiminima (Illa vero quae duas valet minimas, minor vocatur, ut dictum est prius; quae vero sola, minima appellatur; quae vero minimae medietatem, semiminima nominatur [*Philippi de Vitriaco Ars nova*, ed. Gilbert Reaney, André Gilles, and Jean Maillard, Corpus scriptorum de musica, no. 8 ([Rome]: American Institute of Musicology, 1964), p. 24])."

[27]"Yet minimae and semiminimae, at the level at which the minima is placed, can be given other names, so that a minima should be called semiminor and the semiminima should be named the minima (Minimae tamen et semiminimae, ad gradum salvandum in quo posita fuit minima, alia nomina imponi possent, ita quod minima vocetur semiminor et semiminima minima nominetur [ibid])."

[28]*Jacobi Leodiensis Speculum musicae*, 7 vols., ed. Roger Bragard, Corpus scriptorum de musica, no. 3/1–7 ([Rome]: American Institute of Musicology, 1955–1973), 7:65–79.

[29]See chapter 5, *De figuris nominandis* and *De minima* found in de Muris's *Notitia artis musicae* and *Compendium musicae practicae* respectively (de Muris, *Notitia* [ed. Michels]).

remains suspect, as is illustrated by its omission in Johannes Boen's *Ars musicae* of 1357.[30]

The problem with the semiminima is a logical one, for if the minima in its essence is the smallest duration possible, as its name clearly states, how can a smaller note exist? The French, consciously or subconsciously, sidestepped this question throughout the fourteenth century by avoiding the semiminima wherever possible, as is shown by the paucity of semiminimae in the Chantilly codex in comparison to the Modena. The *Tractatus* tries to appease both sides by agreeing that there can be no note smaller than the minima, but arguing that the semiminima is actually a type of minima, varying from it in quality, not essence. Through this argument, the author justifies in theory what he must use in practice.

In light of inconclusive evidence, we must leave the *Tractatus figurarum* as yet another anonymous medieval treatise. At best, we can say that it was most likely written by an Italian trained in the French style in the third quarter of the fourteenth century. The composer Philippus de Caserta would be an ideal candidate for authorship based on these criteria, yet the notation of his extant compositions contradicts this possibility. We must keep in mind, however, the possibility of scribal alterations to notation in the copying of a manuscript and the haphazard survival of sources from this period. Thus, we acknowledge the possibility that the attribution to Philippus by Frater Bonadies and the anonymous commentary in the Seville manuscript may be correct.

The Evolution of the Tractatus's Notation

Passing from the question of authorship to the treatise itself, we are impressed with the clarity and cohesiveness of the *Tractatus figurarum*. Each chapter is carefully built upon the one before, eventually culminating in the problem of notating simultaneous performance of any two of the four mensurations. The author clearly took great pains in the organization of his treatise, and this organic development will be followed in our commentary.

From its first sentence, the *Tractatus figurarum* makes plain the need it is filling. It is a treatise on *figurae*, or noteshapes, through which one can discant in a mensuration different from the tenor, and in the chapters that follow, a convincing and eloquent case is made for the author's new *figurae*. An evolutionary approach to notation is suggested in the prologue, in which two

---

[30]*Ars (musicae) Johannis Boen,* ed. F. Alberto Gallo, Corpus scriptorum de musica, no. 19 ([Rome]: American Institute of Musicology, 1972).

earlier styles of composition are identified. The first and simplest style is exemplified by Philippe de Vitry's motet *Tribum que non abhorruit*. The second—created through the abandonment of the earlier style by the very people who invented it once they had developed a more subtle way—is exemplified by the motet *Apta caro*. The author goes on to state that since his generation has inherited what the two earlier styles left behind, greater subtleties can be accomplished, and what was left imperfect by his predecessors can be perfected by those following.

The two musical examples mentioned in the prologue survive. The first is a motet by Philippe de Vitry, a most fitting place to start since de Vitry's own work, the *Ars nova*, suggests a new style in music. *Tribum que non abhorruit*[31] is a simple three-part isorhythmic motet. Its brief talea in the second mode is stated twelve times and the color twice. Indeed, the occasional parallel perfect consonances and simple rhythmic pattern of the tenor are reminiscent of the previous generation of motets preserved in the Montpellier codex.[32] Of most likely interest to the author of the *Tractatus figurarum* were the groups of undifferentiated semibreves in the cantus and countertenor. The revolution in notation begun by Franco's use of mensural notation to replace neumatic groupings was extended by de Vitry in his *Ars nova*, by whose system composers were freed not only from neumatic groupings but also the rhythmic patterns they enforced. In his system, the old rhythmic modes were replaced by a set of five mensurations used to interpret groups of undifferentiated semibreves. At this time, the semibrevis minima, or minima, had not yet received its characteristic ascending tail. If de Vitry's instructions on the identification of mode are followed, *Tribum que non abhorruit* is revealed to be in imperfect tempus with minor prolation, one of the first pieces to be so identified.[33]

---

[31]See *The Roman de Fauvel, The Works of Philippe de Vitry, French Cycles of the Ordinarium Missae,* ed. Leo Schrade, Polyphonic Music of the Fourteenth Century, vol. 1 (Monaco: Éditions de l'Oiseau-Lyre, 1956), pp. 54–56.

[32]Montpellier, Faculté de médecine, H 196.

[33]It is true that later copies of *Tribum* are notated in imperfect tempus with major prolation, but the earliest known copy, that contained in the *Roman de Fauvel,* is notated in undifferentiated semibreves by whose number imperfect tempus with minor prolation is implied.

The second motet, *Apta caro*,[34] appears to have been quite popular, as is seen from its survival in four separate manuscripts.[35] Its greater complexity is shown in a number of ways, as for instance in its isorhythmic structure. In this case, the talea is much longer and is repeated only three times, stretching over twenty-seven breves in a complex rhythmic pattern. And although no complicated patterns emerge in the upper voices, the cantus is filled with extended passages of minimae and there is a good bit of hocket between it and the triplum as well. This work is listed in the table of contents of the manuscript Trémoïlle and so must have been written before 1376.[36] On the basis of its style and inclusion in such manuscripts as the Durham and Ivrea,[37] Ursula Günther dates it circa 1360.[38]

In comparing these two motets, we begin to see the development of which the author of the *Tractatus* was speaking. *Tribum que non abhorruit* is an excellent example of composition around 1320, written by the most illustrious musician of his day. In it are seen the beginnings of isorhythm, the use of undifferentiated groupings of semibreves, and the use of imperfect tempus, if not prolation. The second motet, *Apta caro*, was composed roughly midcentury and demonstrates a new complexity in its isorhythm. Moreover, in contrast to *Tribum*, whose minimae were most likely undifferentiated from semibreves as to shape, the minima has acquired its final form (that of a semibrevis with an ascending tail) and is well used. Complex rhythmic patterns caused by the simultaneous performance of two or more of the four mensurations still has not occurred. And since this is the goal of the *Tractatus figurarum*, it is apparent that this is the next step the author sees in the evolution of notation.

The Theory of the Tractatus

In chapters 1–5, the tools are presented with which the author will create his new *figurae*, or noteshapes. Chapters 1–2 present the *figurae* accepted at

---

[34]Ursula Günther, *The Motets of the Manuscript Chantilly, Musée Condé, 564 (olim 1047) and Modena, Biblioteca Estense, α.M.5.24 (olim lat. 568)*, Corpus mensurabilis musicae, vol. 39 (Rome: American Institute of Musicology, 1965), pp. 8–13.

[35]Ibid., p. xxv.

[36]Ibid.

[37]Durham, Cathedral Library, C.I.20; Ivrea, Biblioteca Capitolare (without shelf-mark).

[38]Günther, *The Motets*, p. xxv.

the time the *Tractatus* was written, and chapters 3–5 articulate the principles needed in order to manipulate them.

There are five noteshapes in the list of *figurae* left to the then current generation: the duplex longa, longa, brevis, semibrevis, and minima. The list itself is uninteresting; it is merely an enumeration of acceptable *figurae* established by the authority of the period, Johannes de Muris.[39] What is fascinating, however, is the absence of the semiminima from this list, especially since it will be the backbone of the proposed system. The problem inherent with the semiminima and the author's sidestepping of this issue have already been noted. Since he considered the semiminima to be a type of minima, varying from it in quality rather than essence, perhaps he felt it was included in the list under the heading of the minima.

The author closes chapter 2 with an elaboration of the problem he is trying to address. In it, he lists the four mensurations his generation inherited: perfect tempus with major prolation, imperfect tempus with major prolation, perfect tempus with minor prolation, and imperfect tempus with minor prolation. Yet, he points out, his generation was not taught how to combine perfect tempus with minor prolation and imperfect tempus with minor prolation. This combination indeed poses a problem, for it is not the simple combination of imperfect tempus with major prolation and perfect tempus with minor prolation that was in use at the time of Philippe de Vitry and denoted by red notation.[40] Rather, this is a combination of two mensurations based on different numbers of minimae, and so a proportional relationship must be established between the two.

---

[39] de Muris, *Notitia* (ed. Michels), pp. 78–79, 119–34.

[40] "Qua de causa rubeae notulae ponantur in motetis, ne id solum videamur ignorasse, breviter videamus. Dicendum est igitur quod principaliter duabus de causis ponuntur. Vel quia rubeae de alia mensura quam nigrae cantantur, ut in *Thoma tibi obsequia,* quare in tenore illius moteti rubeae cantantur ex temporibus perfectis de modo imperfecto, nigrae vero e converso ... (de Vitry, *Ars nova* [ed. Reaney et al.], p. 28) (For what reason red notes are used in motets, lest we seem to be ignorant of it, we will see shortly. It must be said, therefore, that they are placed principally for two reasons. Either because the red are sung in another mensura than the black, as in *Thoma tibi obsequia*, on which account in the tenor of this motet the red are sung in perfect tempus of imperfect modus and the black conversely ...)."

There follows one of the most startling sentences in the *Tractatus*:

> Quia esset multum inconveniens quod illud quod potest pronuntiari non posset scribi et clare ostendere tractatum hunc parvulum ordinare curavi (72.1–2).[41]

The *Ars subtilior* has often been called a time of theoretical excess in which music was produced laden with complexity and clever effects through the overzealousness of composers, yet here the opposite side is presented. The author is developing his complex set of *figurae* not in order to expand the theoretical frontiers of notation but in response to what is already being performed. It is clear, then, that the impetus for the *Ars subtilior* came not from theorists and composers alone but also from a highly polished group of performers who were rapidly expanding their rhythmic technique.

Having established the *figurae* he will need, the author moves to the principles necessary to manipulate them. Chapter 3 presents a brief summary of these and their use: augmentation and diminution. In the elaboration of the process of diminution (chapter 4), no change is made to the process itself, but it is applied to two *figurae* not considered imperfectable. The discussion of one of these, the minima, is deferred to chapter 6, where the process of diminution is actually applied to a group of minimae. The author concludes this chapter, however, with the hollowing out of the dot of addition. The hollow dot proves itself indispensable to the later manipulation of the *figurae* but has no precedent in any extant theoretical literature.[42] Nor does it appear in any extant music.

The discussion of the hollow dot contained in chapter 4 (78.1–9) is one of the most confusing in the *Tractatus figurarum*.[43] The author begins by stating

---

[41]"Because it would be very incongruous for that which can be performed not to be able to be written, I took care to organize this little treatise to exhibit this clearly."

[42]In a fifteenth-century reworking of Boen's treatise *Ars musicae* (Venezia, Biblioteca Nazionale Marciana, lat. VIII/24 [= 3434]), an example of a hollow dot does occur (see *Ars [musicae]* [ed. Gallo], p. 41). According to the author, miraculous *figurae* were invented by a certain Gwilgon. One of these *figurae* is the semidragma, a dragma half filled and half hollow, having a flag on each stem and followed by a hollow dot. Two of these are supposedly worth three, but three of what? This is never mentioned. The examples given appear corrupt, and it is difficult to tell if a hollow dot was meant at all.

[43]This passage was apparently confusing to the fourteenth century as well, as can be seen by the many copyists' emendations to these sentences.

that when the dot is made hollow, it loses half its value and not a third, as is true of the duplex longa, longa, brevis, and semibrevis, for there is nothing smaller than the dot. The dot loses only half its value because it is a *minus corpus*, which by definition is divisible into only two parts. This position apparently derives from de Vitry's discussion of the *semibrevis major, minor*, and *minima*,[44] for here *minor* is defined as something that is divisible into two parts. This explanation is repeated later (78.5–9), to which the author adds that this dot is not only *minor* but is also to be divided into two semiminimae. The author points out that the dot of addition varies in duration from a brevis to a minima depending upon the note to which it is affixed and that the dot he is discussing is the one worth a minima. At this point, like the minima itself, the dot has a *minor valor* and so is divisible into only two parts: that is, two semiminimae. Thus, if it is made hollow, it can lose only half its value and so be worth one semiminima. Aside from the peculiarity of the hollow dot itself, the author contradicts his own argument later in the *Tractatus*. The proof depends upon the minima being a *minor valor*, or something that is divisible into two parts. In chapter 6 (88.6–7), however, the author makes the minima mensurable—that is, divisible into three parts—and in so doing not only contradicts his earlier demonstration but also traditional French theory on the mensurability of the minima.

Chapter 5 is to contain the discussion of augmentation, but it soon becomes apparent that only augmentation by the addition of a semiminima is of real interest to the author. He begins by saying one need only mention augmentation of the brevis and smaller values, for some sort of confusion would result if a singer had to hold a note longer than this. He immediately moves into a discussion of the semiminima, "because no music is made without it."[45] His basic demonstration of the existence of the semiminima is quite simple: he agrees there can be no note smaller than the minima, but argues that there are various types of minimae. Just as the notes in a ligature are augmented or diminished by means of propriety, so a minima can be augmented or diminished as well. He then points out that through this value (either in the form of a semiminima or a hollow dot) added to other *figurae*, one can discant in a mensuration different from the tenor.

It is interesting to note that the theoretical problems inherent in the semiminima were still controversial as late as the beginning of the fifteenth cen-

---

[44]"That semibrevis which is worth two minimae is called minor ... (Illa [semibrevis] vero quae duas valet minimas, minor vocatur ... [de Vitry, *Ars nova* (ed. Reaney et al.), p. 24])."

[45]See 80.7–8.

tury. In his extensive commentary on Johannes de Muris's *Tractatus cantus mensurabilis*[46] written in 1404, Prosdocimo de' Beldomandi must add a lengthy section following de Muris's list of *figurae* to justify the semiminima, for the semiminima does not appear on that list. In the following discussion, he summarizes current thought on the semiminima in which he includes the reasoning given in the *Tractatus figurarum*.[47] Prosdocimo, however, objects to this argument as false on the analogy of the semibrevis: if this argument were true, the semibrevis would be a type of brevis and not an independent note value at all.[48] It is unfortunate that the *Tractatus figurarum* relied so heavily upon the semiminima, for this could, to a large extent, explain the system's ultimate failure.

The Figurae

Having completed the description of both the basic *figurae* and the means of manipulating them, the author then presents his new *figurae* arranged in rhythmic patterns that will be of use in the final four chapters on the four mensurations. In this way, nothing new appears in the final chapters, for the value and derivation of each group of *figurae* has already been demonstrated.

---

[46]*Expositiones tractatus pratice cantus mensurabilis magistri Johannis de Muris*, ed. F. Alberto Gallo, Antiqui musicae italicae scriptores, no. 3: Prodocimi de Beldemandis opera, vol. 1 (Bologna: Antiquae Musicae Italicae Studiosi, 1966).

[47]"Alii vero adhuc aliter respondent concedendo solum quinque esse partes prolationis, scilicet maximam, longam, brevem, semibrevem et minimam. Et dicunt ulterius, quod semiminima a minima non distinguitur, sed sub ipsa comprehenditur tamquam minus comune sub magis comuni. Propter quod dicunt minimam esse duplicem, scilicet minimam maiorem et est illa que sine cauda retorta figuratur, et minimam minorem et est illa quam semiminimam nominamus et que cum cauda retorta figuratur. Et sic volunt utramque istarum sub minima comprehendi (ibid., p. 27) (Still others answer in a different way conceding the parts of prolation to be only five, that is, the maxima, longa, brevis, semibrevis, and minima. And lastly they say that a semiminima is not distinguished from a minima but is included under it as a smaller [value] is commonly [included] under the greater. On account of that, they say that the minima should be of two types, that is, the minima maior [and it is this one that is drawn without a tail turned back on itself] and the minima minor [and it is this one that is named the semiminima and is drawn with a tail turned back on itself]. And so they wish both of them to be included under the minima)."

[48]Ibid.

Each pattern may now be illustrated and its derivation and rhythmic value explained.

◻︎◻︎◻︎

The *Tractatus* states that three hollow breves are to be substituted for two breves of perfect tempus with major prolation, and in this they are unique. All other groups of *figurae* are designed to replace one brevis of another tempus, but this example replaces two. Perhaps this is intended to address a change in modus: if the modus had been imperfect (i.e., one longa equalling two breves), this would create perfect modus (i.e., one longa equalling three breves). Since modus is not a concern of the *Tractatus*, but only the four mensurations, this possibility seems unlikely. It appears that this example is more in accord with the concept of *traynour* discussed at the close of the *Tractatus*.

These *figurae* are substituted for one brevis of perfect tempus with major prolation; in other words, they allow for imperfect tempus in the context of perfect. This is the first *figura* to make use of the principle of the composite noteshape. As is apparent from their description in the *Tractatus*, the upper portion of the *figura* is that of a semibrevis and the lower that of a semiminima. It is curious that the *Tractatus* identifies a perfect, dotted semibrevis as worth four minimae. This is necessary, however, for the *figurae* to add up correctly: each of the *figurae* would then equal four minimae and a semiminima, or four-and-a-half minimae, and so together would add up to nine—the number of minimae in one brevis of perfect tempus with major prolation.

◆·◆·

This is an example of the perfection of imperfect semibreves through the dot of perfection (useful in notating imperfect tempus in the context of perfect tempus with minor prolation).

Each of these notes is said to be worth an imperfect semibrevis: that is, two minimae. This is the second example of the use of composite noteshapes, with each *figura* being the conflation of two minimae. This notation contradicts practice as documented by the Berkeley Manuscript,[49] which contains the writings of a theorist trained in the French style around 1375,[50] who states that a descending tail added to a note increases its value by one-half.[51] The two *figurae*, strictly speaking, are not the same, for the *Tractatus*'s noteshape is a combination of two minimae while the Berkeley Manuscript's noteshape is a minima with a descending tail. Their appearance is the same, however, and both appear in the music of the period. In any case, according to the *Tractatus*, these *figurae* are used in imperfect tempus with major prolation to notate perfect tempus.

These *figurae* are created by hollowing out the previous set, and so they lose one third of their value and are equivalent to four minimae. They are used in imperfect tempus with minor prolation to notate perfect tempus.

According to the *Tractatus*, these *figurae* are called imperfect minimae, once again implying that the minima can be imperfected and is mensurable. They are explained as being of greater effect than semiminimae because they are solid, but of lesser effect than minimae because they have the sign (i.e., the flag) of semiminimae. Four of these imperfect minimae replace three perfect minimae but are never used as such in the system presented. In this form,

---

[49]"These sorts of figures were invented: [example], and they are referred to as fusa by musicians; two of these commonly replace three minimae in both prolations (Item inventi sunt hii modi figurarum: [exempla], et sunt a musicis fusa nuncupata, quarum due ponuntur pro tribus minimis communiter et utriusque prolacionis [Oliver B. Ellsworth, ed., *The Berkeley Manuscript*, Greek and Latin Music Theory, vol. 2 (Lincoln: University of Nebraska Press, 1984), pp. 126–27])."

[50]Ibid., pp. 1, 11.

[51]"Just as an upward tail always lightens by half, so a tail pointing down (in the opposite direction) ought to become heavy by half; and if one pointing up should diminish, one in the opposite direction ought to augment (Nam sicut cauda sursum alleviat aliquando pro medietate, sic cauda deorsum tendens debet pro medietate per oppositum aggravari, et si sursum tendens tollat per oppositum deorsum debet augere [ibid., pp. 126–29])."

they can be used to produce octonaria in imperfect tempus with major prolation or in perfect tempus with minor prolation, or to produce duodenaria in perfect tempus with major prolation. The author is not unconcerned here with the Italian *divisiones*; imperfect minimae are indispensable, though, in the composite *figurae* to be discussed later.

The imperfect minima is not unique to the *Tractatus figurarum*; it appears in other fourteenth-century sources under the name *additae*.[52] The more common way of denoting this rhythmic grouping is with four hollow red minimae or the reversed C mensuration sign.

The author then turns to a discussion of the use of red notation, making it quite plain that it should only be used in an exchange of imperfect tempus with major prolation and perfect tempus with minor prolation (or contrariwise) and not as a general sign of diminution. He does accept the option, though, of using hollow black notation instead of red if red ink is not available.

These *figurae* are built in a two-step process. First, four minimae and four imperfect minimae are joined, using the principle of composite noteshapes, to create four *figurae* worth seven minimae. To these are applied hollow dots, each equivalent to a seminima, and so the four *figurae* add up to nine minimae. This elaborate set of *figurae* is used to notate imperfect tempus with minor prolation in the context of perfect tempus with major prolation.

By the combination of two minimae and two semiminimae, these *figurae* result and are used in notating minor prolation while in major, the two notes equalling three minimae. This rhythm is more commonly denoted in the music of the time by two minimae with descending tails, where the descending tail will add half a note's value. In any case, the two processes produce the same result.

---

[52]"Nevertheless, the following sorts of figures were invented: [example], four of which commonly replace three minimae and are called *additae* (Tamen inventi sunt infrascripti modi figurarum: [exempla], quarum 4 communiter ponuntur pro tribus minimis, et vocantur addite [ibid., pp. 124–25])."

In this set, there is no sidestepping the issue of the mensurability of the minima. The author clearly states that a hollow minima will lose one third its value, and these three hollow minimae are therefore equivalent to two solid minimae. In order for the minima to lose one third its value, it must be divisible by three and thus mensurable. At this point the author contradicts both himself and standard theory as well. In the section on the hollow dot, pains were taken to show the minima as a *minor valor* and so divisible by two, a concept necessary if the hollow dot is to equal a semiminima. Here, that concept is contradicted. If the minima is to be a *minor valor*, it must be divisible by two, but if it is mensurable, it is divisible by three. The immensurability of the minima was established by Philippe de Vitry, who stated that the minima was equivalent to two semiminimae.[53] The *figurae* of this set are necessary in order to change minor prolation to major, but in so doing, the author allows a second point of controversy into his system.[54]

Having completed his inventory of rhythmic patterns, the author moves to their use in the four mensurations. Each mensuration is given its own chapter in which the appropriate rhythmic patterns are shown for performing in the other three. Little new information is added here, since all the patterns have previously been explained in the chapter preceding these. Nevertheless, one impossible situation does arise.

In the final chapter, which concerns imperfect tempus with minor prolation, the author points out the impossibility of discanting in perfect tempus with major prolation (while in imperfect tempus with minor prolation) because of the equivalence of the *minimae*. The author reminds us that minimae can only be divided into semiminimae (again contradicting himself) and so the four minimae that compose imperfect tempus with minor prolation will increase to eight, one short of the nine needed for perfect tempus with major

---

[53]"That which is worth two minimae is called minor, as was said earlier; [that] which [is worth] one is named minima; [that] which [is worth] half of a minima is named semiminima (Illa vero quae duas valet minimas, minor vocatur, ut dictum est prius; quae vero sola, minima appellatur; quae vero minimae medietatem, semiminima nominatur [de Vitry, *Ars nova* (ed. Reaney et al.), p. 24])." "And if they should be divided, they would be divided through semiminimae, each minima of which is divided into two semiminimae (Et si dividantur, per semiminimas dividentur, quarum quaelibet minima in duas dividitur semiminimas [ibid., p. 30])."

[54]The first was that of the semiminima.

prolation. The only alternative offered is to notate in perfect tempus with minor prolation, since perfect tempus with major prolation is an impossibility.

The chapter closes with the typical formula:

> Sic itaque ad complementum huius operis consecutus sum ideo refero gratias deo, Amen (98.8–9).[55]

The Epilogue

This statement could reasonably be taken as the close of the *Tractatus figurarum*, yet nearly all sources contain a postscript in which the concept of *traynour* is discussed. The few manuscripts that omit this section have no apparent relationship to each other, while some of the earliest datable sources already contain it. Although the passage may not have survived in all copies of the *Tractatus figurarum*, its importance warrants inclusion in this edition. Moreover, it fits very well with the main body of the text, both in style and notation.

The concept of *traynour* is not new with the *Tractatus figurarum*; it appears already in the *Quatuor principalia musicae*.[56] This treatise is a compilation of musical theory edited at Oxford by a Franciscan monk from Bristol, who preferred to remain anonymous.[57] The work has been dated 1351, but this is questionable because the early date does not well accord with a topic of the *ars subtilior* such as *traynour*.[58] In any event, *treyn* is mentioned in a section explaining how four minimae cannot be sung in the time of three.[59] The theoretical reasoning states that in this case, there is no equipollence on any level, beyond that which is forcibly created from the superposition of voices. On a more practical level, the author observes that in performance either a rest will be added to the group of three or one note of the group of three will be doubled in value so that both groups, in effect, will be of the same duration. It is this type of complexity that the author calls *tractus* (a dragging) or *treyns* (from the French *trainer* [?]—to drag) or *sincopa*. *Sincopa* is defined by Johannes de Muris as the splitting of a group of notes that together form a

---

[55]"As I have come to the completion of this work, I therefore give thanks to God, Amen."

[56]CS, 4:200–298.

[57]Gilbert Reaney, "The Question of Authorship in the Medieval Treatises on Music," *Musica Disciplina* 18 (1964): 10.

[58]Ibid., p. 11.

[59]For a complete transcription of this chapter, see CS, 4:277.

perfection.[60] The concept of dragging accords quite well with *sincopa*, in which the tempus is displaced in one voice and remains displaced until brought back in line when the displaced perfection is completed. Another possible meaning comes from the Latin *tractus*, which is something drawn. This word is used in the phrase *tractatus verborum*, a drawling in pronunciation, and is certainly a descriptive term for the aural effect caused by singing the complex rhythmic pattern of four notes against three.

By the time the *Tractatus figurarum* was written, the concept of *traynour* and *sincopa* had separated, for the *Tractatus* states that *traynour* is a more energetic (*fortior*) style than *sincopare*. It is unclear exactly what the author means by *fortior*, but some sort of increase in intensity is obviously required. From the few examples given following this statement, the concept as presented in the *Tractatus figurarum* appears more in line with an intensified form of *sincopa* than a complex superpositioning of rhythms. In *sincopa*, all parts are in the same mensuration; only the downbeat, as it were, has been shifted for a time in one of the parts. In *traynour*, however, the parts are in mensurations of differing lengths. Until this point, the *Tractatus figurarum* explained the superimposition of different mensurations on the basis of an equal brevis. Now, to the contrary, mensurations are combined using only the equivalence of the minima, allowing the basic tempus units to be of differing lengths. In this case, an alignment of the mensurations will only occur every few tempora. This concept is similar to that of syncopation in that the tempora of the various parts do not always align, but in the former case, this occurs through the displacement of the same mensuration, while in the latter, it occurs through the cyclic combination of mensurations of varying lengths. The following examples appear in the final section of the *Tractatus*.[61]

---

[60]"Sincopa est divisio cujuscunque figure per partes separatas, que numerando perfectiones ad invicem reducuntur, et potest fieri in modo, tempore, et prolatione (CS, 3:56) (*Sincopa* is the division of any *figura* you wish into separate parts, which are reduced one to another by numbering perfections, and it can be done in modus, tempus, and prolatio [cf. *Berkeley Manuscript* (ed. Ellsworth), pp. 176–77])."

[61]For a description of the extended sets of examples found in Se1, see the Appendix.

De tempore perfecto majoris

The void notation in the example is equivalent to the three hollow breves given in 90.8, but in this case the hollow breves have been broken up into nine hollow semibreves. It is impossible to align the two parts brevis-for-brevis, but alignment will occur after a group of three hollow breves (or nine hollow semibreves) set against two filled breves.

De tempore perfecto minoris

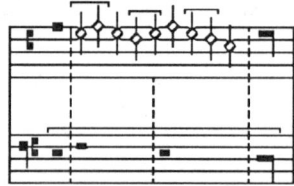

This example is identical to the previous one, except it is now in perfect tempus with minor prolation. The same *figurae* are used that, according to the *Tractatus*, should be used to discant in perfect tempus with minor prolation against imperfect tempus with minor prolation (96.13–15). The author was obviously not against using a *figura* merely for its rhythmic value in other contexts.

De tempore imperfecto majoris

In the next two examples, the situation becomes more complex. The use of three hollow semibreves is prescribed in the *Tractatus* (94.4–5) to change the tempus of this mensuration from imperfect to perfect, yet if this were all that was meant, there would be no need for this example at this time. Following the lead of the two previous examples, it becomes clear that hollow semibreves are needed to set up the same pattern in this mensuration. In this case, they must be grouped as three groups of two and not two groups of three.

De tempore imperfecto minoris

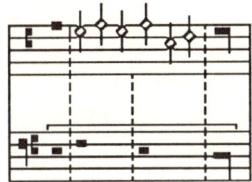

This example exactly parallels the former. Again, the *figurae* used are defined as changing the tempus from imperfect to perfect, yet they can also be grouped in three groups of two and so are similar to the other examples of *traynour*.

De semibrevibus perfectis

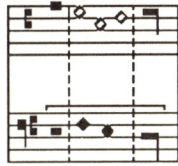

This final example does not appear to be consistent with the others. If, however, we consider this to be an example of augmentation in which the semibrevis replaces the brevis as the main unit, it does indeed parallel the other examples.

With these few examples of *traynour*, the *Tractatus figurarum* draws to a close, having revealed a number of important theoretical concepts from the end of the fourteenth century. First of all, we see the continuing problem surrounding the semiminima. Although it was mentioned in Philippe de Vitry's *Ars nova* at the beginning of the century, it was not recognized by the century's leading theorist, Johannes de Muris. Related to this controversy is that of the mensurability of the minima. In order for the *Tractatus*'s hollow dot to be equal to a semiminima, the minima must be a *minor valor*, that is, divisible by two and thus immensurable. Later in the treatise, however, the minima is made hollow, something that is only possible if it can lose a third of its value—or is mensurable. This internal flaw of the *Tractatus figurarum* may indeed be responsible for its ultimate rejection.

Second, the principle of composite noteshapes is revealed, for it is clear that many of the rather oddly formed *figurae* are merely the union of two different noteshapes in one body. This process goes far in explaining the origin of some of the other fantastically shaped *figurae* in use at this time and gives a means for unravelling their true rhythmic value.

Third, one sees the continued use of red notation in its original context: that is, introducing perfect tempus with minor prolation into imperfect tempus with major prolation or the contrary. It has been assumed that red notation became a general sign of diminution and that hollow black notation was a ready substitute. But there are examples of late fourteenth-century notation that make use of both red and hollow black notation. The *Tractatus*, then, not only shows the need for both—the hollow black being used as a sign of diminution outside the function of the red—but also reveals, in the case of red notation, what mensurations are being used in the composition at that point.

Indirect evidence is given by the *Tractatus'* s use of simultaneous mensurations for the concept of an equal brevis under some circumstances at the end of the fourteenth century. We cannot tell from this how widespread was the practice, only that it must have existed. It is curious that the *Tractatus* combines the concepts of equal minima and equal brevis by creating a complex set of *figurae* through which a performer could mimic a different mensuration, as opposed to an actual change in mensuration in which the common denominator between the two must be clearly stated or understood. It should also be pointed out, however, that in the section on *traynour*, the author gives examples of change in mensuration based only upon the equivalence of the minima where no sense of an equal brevis was desired.

Although the system espoused in the *Tractatus figurarum* did not achieve its goal of integrating the notational multiplicities of the late fourteenth century into one inclusive system, its illustration of certain basic notational principles is important. These principles may be applied to surviving musical sources and help to unravel their notational mysteries, illuminating the notational subtleties in which this music revelled.

The Manuscripts

Ca

Catania, Biblioteche Riunite Civica e Antonio Ursino Recupero, Ursino Recupero D.39[62]

Paper; 248 folios, 26.5x20.5 cm
Sicily or southern Italy; 1473

Title of treatise no. 2, "ILLVMINATOR [*in later hand:* di Barbo Jacobus]" (f. 1r; f. 1v blank)

1. Treatise on geometry (first part [see item 6]). *Inc.* "Geometria assecutiua est arsmetrice et posteriorum ordinis est et passiones numeri …" *Exp.* "… Si placet eam reducere in aliam priorem possumus eam redducere in vltimam omnem scientiam sicut reduximus primam causam de triangulis et reducemus primam de circulis. Sequitur secunda conclusio in antesequentibus foliis xxvj." (unedited) (ff. 2r–8r)

2. Jacobus Barbo, treatise on rhetoric, *Luminator*. *Inc.* "Prologus. Incipit liber luminator. Capitulum 1. CUm ergo in libellis marci tullij ciceronis Virgilijque Terencij Sepius legi et In ceteris Doctoribus in quibus multa inueniuntur graciose posita que ad pulcritudinem loquendi satis sufficiunt …" *Exp.* "… Ego enim Iacobus borbo minimus Inter musicos Adolescentulorum Cappelle alti Alfonsi Regis Magister melius quod potui hunc paruulum libellum ordinauj Sub era domini Millesima Quadringentesima Quinquagesima tercia. Ego enim Supradicti Reuerendissimi magistri borbo humilis Discipulus et Inter clericos Regie Cappelle minimus et Ignorantissimus omnium per preceptum eiusdem Magistri Borbo scripsi et de reseranti stilo in hoc presenti actuli id est de layca lingua in latinam transtuli. Deo gracias Explicit Liber qui uocatur Illuminator Amen. Amen." (F. Alberto Gallo, "Musica, poetica e retorica nel quattrocento: l'*Illuminator* di Giacomo Borbo," *Rivista italiana di musicologia* 10 [1975]: 72–85) (ff. 8r–11v)

3. Goscalcus Francigena, three treatises with introduction. Introduction *inc.* "Quoniam in antelapsis temporibus quamplures de cantibus tam ecclesiasticis quam aliis utpothe de moctetis baladis Rondellis uireletis et aliis atque eorum cognicione pratice Videlicet et speculatiue diuersimode sunt loquuti …" *Exp.* "… Et demum de cognicione notularum

---

[62]This description, with few alterations, has been taken from Prosdocimo de' Beldomandi, *Brevis summula proportionum quantum ad musicam pertinet and Parvus tractatulus de modo monacordum dividendi*, ed. Jan Herlinger, Greek and Latin Music Theory, vol. 4 (Lincoln: University of Nebraska Press, 1987). For full codicological description, see pp. 17–19.

cum suis praticalibus intendo procedere dei gratia mediante." (*Berkeley Manuscript* [ed. Ellsworth], introduction) (f. 12r)

a. On plainchant and tuning. *Inc.* "Cum autem Cognoscere cuius modi siue toni sit quilibet cantus Cantor ipsius noticiam presupponat pro eius cognicione ..." *Exp.* "... Set quia diuideretur tonus tam pro cliesos [*sic*] quam pro comatha que bono modo notarj non possent hic ponere non curaui Et sic est finis primj tractatus per xpistum dominum nostrum. Et sequitur Secundus tractatus de contrapuncto." (*Berkeley Manuscript* [ed. Ellsworth], treatises 1 and 5) (ff. 12r–20r)

b. On counterpoint. *Inc.* "Quoniam Musici antiquorum philosophorum ab vsu discrepare nolentes set intendentes eorum uestigia utpothe clarius directiua posterius imitarj ..." *Exp.* "... Sic igitur de contrapuncto et non nullis etiam ipsum contingentibus puta uocum diuisionibus cum aliquibus suis exemplis et pertinenciis superficialiter declarabo. Cunctis in premissis intellectis et scitis perfecte distancijs artem audire volentes securum iter inuenire uolentes potuerunt et per ea acquirere fundamentum. Et per hoc fit finis secundi tractatus Et sequitur tercius uidelicet de cognicione notularum cum suis pertinencijs." (*Berkeley Manuscript* [ed. Ellsworth], treatise 2) (ff. 20r–24v)

c. On mensuration. *Inc.* "Quilibet Igitur In arte pratica mensurabilis cantus erudiri mediocriter affectans post hec que superius dicta sunt ea scribat diligentius que sequuntur summarie compilata ..." *Exp.* "... Et hec predicta quecunque redduci sufficiant in arte mensurabilis cantus praticam mediocriter anhelantibus Introduci. Et per hec fit finis huius librj comppilati parisius. Anno a natiuitate Dominj Millesimo ccc°lxxv° Die xij° mensis Ianuarij per Eximium Doctorem Gostaltum Francigenam. AMEN." (*Berkeley Manuscript* [ed. Ellsworth], treatise 3) (ff. 24v–30r)

4. Note on Arabic and Roman numerals. *Inc.* "Sequitur numerus alphabeti cum suo numero per versus. 500 Possidet a numerum quingentos ordine recto. a. ccccc ..." *Exp.* "... 2000 Vltimam canit finem bis mille tenere. z. mm. Finis." (unedited) (f. 30v)

5. Note on Roman numerals. *Inc.* "Sequitur numerus ecclesiasticus. I monos v quinos x decem ..." *Exp.* "... Centum l sic numerus debemus scribere totum. Finis." (unedited) (f. 30v)

6. continuation of item 1. *Inc.* "Secunda conclusio. Omne perallelorum angulos ex aduerso collocatos habet equales ..." *Exp.* "... omnis rectilineus differt a recto plusquam sit angulus contingentie igitur angulus semicirculj." (unedited) (ff. 31r–33r)

7. Jacobus Barbo, treatise on ratios. *Inc.* "Jacobus de Barbo. Postquam adimpleti sunt tres libri scilicet primus de Cantu immensurato qui dicitur cantus planus. secundus de cantu mensurato qui organicus appellatur. tercius de contrapuncto qui biscantus vocatur. Nunc restat in hoc quarto et ultimo libro tractare de proporcionibus musicalibus iuxta mei parui possibilitatem ingenij ..." *Exp.* "Proportio maioris inequalitatis est quando maior numerus comparatur minorj. Proportio minoris

inequalitatis est quando minor numerus comperatur maiorj addendo." (based on Prosdocimo's *Proportiones* and collated with it in Prosdocimo de' Beldomandi, *Brevis summula* [ed. Herlinger]) (ff. 33v–34r)

8. Note on solmization. *Inc.* "La fa sol papri ..." *Exp.* "... sol mi fa sol pa sep I mire mi fa palix. Hec ille." (unedited) (f. 34v)

9. Treatise on arithmetic. *Inc.* "Hec algorismus. Presens ars dicitur in qua Talibus Indorum fruimur bis quinque figuris. vt hic 0.9.8.7.6.5.4.3.2.1. ..." *Exp.* "... si continua non sit progressio finis Impar tunc maius medium se multiplicabit. Si par per medium si multiplicato propinquum. DEO GRACIAS." (unedited) (ff. 35r–37v)

10. Note on intervals. *Inc.* "Species cantus sunt hee que sequuntur. Vnus. Vnus sonus. semitonus. Tonus ..." *Exp.* "... omnis Simplex consonantia Infra dyapasson Amplectitur et quicquid exterius est reiteracio vocatur." (unedited) (ff. 38r–39r)

11. Note on text underlay in plainchant. *Inc.* "Nota de locatione uerborum. Ad locandum verba sive partes in canto plano quatuor sunt notanda ..." *Exp.* "... non debet locarj in notulis correptis quas In mensurato cantu semibreues dicimus. DEO GRACIAS." (unedited) (f. 39r)

12. Note on solmization. *Inc.* "Primo sciendum est quod disiuncta est vehemens transitus ex vna deductione in alia absque mutatione uel de vna proprietate in alia ..." *Exp.* "... vbicumque ponitur istud signum ♮ quadrj In linea et in spacio debet alienarj sonus illius articuli per unus [*sic*] maius semitonum et debet dici mi. Et hoc intelligitur per totam palmam vbi Inueniretur fa.mi. ad Intellectum predictum et ista regula Intelligitur quantum ad generales coniunctas." (unedited) (f. 39r–v)

13. Note on psalm tones. *Inc.* "Est sciendum quod psalmi debent Intonarj secundum Auctores musice secundum hos tres modos ..." *Exp.* "... Sol.fa.mi.re.fa ternus Re.ut.re.mi.reque quaternus." (unedited) (ff. 39v–40v)

14. Treatise on counterpoint, *Nota quod contrapunctus est fundamentum biscantus*. *Inc.* "Sequuntur Regule contrapuncti secundum Vsum Regni Sicilie. Nota quod contrapunctus est fundamentum biscantus ..." *Exp.* "... Nota quod vnisonus de omne la. est la. uel re. tercia est fa. uel ut. quinta est la. uel mi. sexta est fa. Octaua est la. uel re. decima est fa. duodecima est la uel mi. tercia decima est fa et quinta decima est la. uel re. et sic ad infinitum." (Paolo Nalli, "Regulae contrapuncti secundi usum Regni Siciliae," *Archivio storico per la Sicilia orientale* 29 [1933]: 287–88) (ff. 40v–41v)

15. Treatise on counterpoint, *Quoniam latens scientia*. *Inc.* "SEQVUNTUR REGVLE CONTRAPVNCTI. Quoniam Latens scientia nichil prodest et cito labitur distributa autem per oppositum multum prodest et magnum recipit Incrementum ..." *Exp.* "... que requiruntur ad eius bonitatem sunt quatuor. scilicet biscantus uel contrapunctus debet esse pulcrior per se. secundo absque reditas notas.

tercio ex specie non geminata. quarto consonantias sic graduatas." (Nalli, "Regulae contrapuncti," pp. 288–91) (f. 41v)

16. Treatise on counterpoint, *Primo sciendum est quod duodecim. Inc.* "Sequitur quomodo contrapunctus debet ordinarj. PRimo sciendum est quod duodecim sunt Species biscantus Scilicet vnisonus, tercia. quinta. Sexta. octaua ..." *Exp.* "... quo tendis Ire propinquiorem debes accipere. Hec ille. [table of consonances]" (Nalli, "Regulae contrapuncti," pp. 291–92) (ff. 41v–42v)

17. Note on modes. *Inc.* "Primus tonus habet cordam in F. et finit tercius subtus regulam In d. et habet semitonum subtus regulam In e. ..." *Exp.* "... Octauus tonus habet cordam. in g. et finit ibidem et habet semitonium mediate tercius [?] subtus regulam In e gravj et aliud semitonium tercius subtus regulam mediate In ♮ quadro." (unedited) (f. 43r)

18. Two poems
    a. On text underlay. *Inc.* "Sillaba cum fuerit notis subiecta duabus | Sub prima resonat Incipiatque sonus ..." *Exp.* "... Set cum correptis dabitur transgressio notis | Sillaba principium nequit habere suum." (unedited) (f. 43r)
    b. On singing the Gloria Patri. *Inc.* "Gregorium sequere quom reddere gloria patrj | Contendes lector pandet tibi regula presens. ..." *Exp.* "... Sol la. sol sexta sol mi. fa. sol. septima fiet | Mi re. mi resonet gloria cum repperit octo." (unedited) (f. 43v)

19. Boethius, *Musica. Inc.* "[O]mnium quidem percepcio sensuum ita sponte ac naturaliter quibusdam viuentibus adest ..." *Exp.* "... Dispocio diuersorum generum cum numeris et proporcionibus Dyatonici equalis ptholomej diuisio etc. Amen. EXPLICIT LIBER BOECIJ DE MVSICA ID EST ARMONICA. Completum est presens opus per me Matheum de collitortis De Castro Johannis Anno Domini Millesimo cc°cc lxxiij° Mense octobris Sexto die mensis eiusdem Septimi Indicionis." (*Anicii Manlii Torquati Severini Boetii De institutione arithmetica libri duo, de institutione musica libri quinque*, ed. Gottfried Friedlein [Leipzig: Teubner, 1867; reprint ed., Frankfort: Minerva, 1966]) (ff. 44r–115v)

20. Tables of notes and intervals, showing a chromatic scale with four sharps and five flats as well as A-sharp in the lowest octave and C-flat in the two upper octaves, in Pythagorean tuning (appendix D in Prosdocimo de' Beldomandi, *Brevis summula* [ed. Herlinger], pp. 139–47) (f. 116r–v)

21. Note on the power of music. *Inc.* "Musica est domina continens omnium methadorum principia ..." *Exp.* "... nutriens amorem. honorans possessorem in finem debitum fuit ad dei laudem finaliter est inuenta." (unedited) (f. 117r)

22. Johannes de Muris, *Libellus cantus mensurabilis. Inc.* "Incipit pratica magistri Johannis de muris. Quislibet In arte pratica mensurabilis can-

tus debet esse eruditus et affectans erudirj: ea scribat diligenter. que sequntur. summarie compilata secundum Magistrum Iohannem de muris ..." *Exp.* "... Et predicta quamuis rudea sufficiunt In arte mensurabilis de uellantibus introducti." (CS, 3:46–58) (ff. 117r–121v)

23. Treatise on trecento mensuration, *Capitulum de modo accipiendo*. *Inc.* "De modo accipiendo. Nota quod modus accipitur a longa. Tempus a breuj Et prolacio a semibreuj...." *Exp.* "... Set in cantu reducuntur ad modum quaternarium dicitur de prolacione minori inperfecta hoc modo quia maior que ponitur in modo duodenario et per talem reductionem perficitur longa. Et eodem modo videmus de octonario." (*Mensurabilis musicae tractatuli* [ed. Gallo], p. 59) (ff. 121v–122r)

24. Treatise on mensuration. *Inc.* "Quid sit prolacio ..." *Exp.* "... sufficientur sic ut patet [?]." (f. 122r)

25. *Tractatus figurarum*. *Inc.* "Quoniam sicut domino placuit sciencia musice in corde desiderancium gloriose perlustrauit ..." *Exp.* "... quia ascenderet usque ad octo et numerus sic deficeret sicque ad complementum huius operis consecutus. Ideo refero semper gratias deo. Amen." (ff. 122r–123v)

26. Treatise on ratios. *Inc.* "Incipit tractatus proporcionum. Duppla proporcio est quando maior numerus continet totum minorem numerum bis ut 2. ad 1. 4. ad 2. 6. ad 3. et sic in infinitum ..." *Exp.* "... Proporcio tripla sexquiquarta est quando maior numerus continet minorem ter et eius quartam partem ut 13. ad 4. 26 ad 8. Et sic In Infinitum numerum. Sit laus et gloria xpisto per Infinita seculorum secula. Amen." (unedited) (ff. 123v–125r; f. 125v blank)

27. Roger Caperon, *Comentum super cantum*. *Inc.* "Incipit comentum magistri Rogerij caperonij anglici super cantum. [U]t ad doctrinam artis musice. venire possimus ..." *Exp.* "... per constitutas neque enim per predictas mutaciones consona ac regulariter decantarj non [?] potest [*example with music:* Exurge domine. fer xpisti nobis et libera nos pro(p)ter nomen tuum]." (unedited) (ff. 126ra–155rb)

28. Commentary on Boethius, *Musica*. *Inc.* "Primus quidem liber qui incipit: Omnium quidem percepcio etc...." *Exp.* "... Ekmioles non sunt que non recipiunt in consonanciarum coniunctione et sunt que opponuntur ex equisonis et consonis ut dyapason cum dyathesaron et similes. Explicit summa boecij." (unedited) (ff. 155va–156vb)

29. Marchetto, *Lucidarium*. *Inc.* "[M]agnifico militi et potenti: Domino Domino suo Raynerio ..." *Exp.* "... musicus. sentit. desinit. eligit. ordinat et disponit que ipsam tangunt scienciam et per cantorem Iubet tanquam per suum nuncium praticarj. Et hec de musica plana sufficiant ibi dicta. Explicit Lucidarium magistri Marqueti de padua. Sit laus semper et gloria xpisto. Amen." (*The Lucidarium of Marchetto of Padua: A Critical Edition, Translation, and Commentary*, ed. Jan Herlinger [Chicago: University of Chicago Press, 1985]) (ff. 157ra–189rb; f. 189v blank)

30. Prosdocimo, *Expositiones tractatus pratice cantus mensurabilis magistri Johannis de Muris. Inc.* "Rogasti me amice dilecte ut In arte musicali tui amore aliqua in uno opusculo colligerem ..." *Exp.* "... et per hoc Infallanter in noticiam mensurare cuiuscumque cantus tibi proposti deuenire poteris si laborare uolueris et sic fit finis tocius huius operis prosdocimus [*sic*] de beldomandis pactauum. Anno Domini Millesimo cccc° xij° padue compilati [?]." (Prosdocimo de' Beldomandi, *Expositiones* [ed. Gallo]) (ff. 190ra–241rb)

31. Prosdocimo, *Brevis summula proportionum quantum ad musicam pertinet. Inc.* "Tibi dilecte frater tuus prosdocimus de beldomandis pactauus de nocte laborauit ..." *Exp.* "... nisi ut additionem Ipsius nec sub denotant comparationem minoris quantitatis ad maiorem. Et hec ergo sunt que habuj loqui summatis [?] tibi de proportionibus musice applicantibus etc. Deo gracias. Expeditum est hoc opus anno Domini Millesimo cccc° lxxiij° mense decembris xv° die eiusdem mensis vij° indictionis ad instanciam clerici antonij de russo Cantoris eximij." (Prosdocimo de' Beldomandi, *Brevis summula* [ed. Herlinger]) (ff. 241rb–242vb; f. 243r blank)

32. Excerpts from Isidore, *Etymologiae* (*Isidori Hispalensis Episcopi Etymologiarum sive originum libri XX*, 2 vols., ed. W. M. Lindsay [Oxford: Clarendon, 1911], vol. 1).

    a. 3.1–9, on arithmetic. *Inc.* "De uocabulo arismetrice discipline. De auctoribus eius. Quid sit numerus. Quid prestent numeri. De prima diuisione parium et imparium. De secunda diuisione tocius numeri. De tercia diuisione tocius numeri. De diferencia arismetrice. geometrie et musice artis. Quid numeri Infiniti existunt. De arismetrica. Arismetrica est disciplina numerorum Greci enim numerum rithmon uocant ..." *Exp.* "... Ita vero suis quisque numerus proprietatibus terminatur ut nullus eorum par esse cuicunque alteri possit ergo et dispares inter se atque diuersi et singuli quique finiti sunt et omnes Infiniti sunt." (ff. 243va–245vb)

    b. 3.10–13, on geometry. *Inc.* "Incipit liber 5 de geometria. De inuentoribus geometrie. De quadripartita diuisione geometrie. De uocabulo eius. De figuris. De numeris. Geometrie disciplina primum ab egepcijs reperta dicitur quod Invndante nilo et omnium post omnibus limo abductis ..." *Exp.* "... 6 et 12 multiplicata faciunt septuagies dipondius Media 8 et 9 multiplicata tantundem faciunt." (ff. 245vb–246rb)

    c. 3.15–23, on music. *Inc.* "Capitula sexti libri. De nomine musice. de prima diuisione musice. Que armonia dicitur. De inuentoribus eius. De secunda diuisione que organica uocatur. Quid possit esse musica. De tercia que rithimica nuncupatur. De tribus partibus musice. De numeris musicis. De triformi musice diuisione. Incipit liber 6 de musica. Musica est pericia modulacionis sono cantuque conscistens ..." *Exp.* "... eiusdem musice perfectionem et metra consistunt In arys et thesys id est In eleuacione et posicione." (ff. 246rb–248rb)

33. Notes on arithmetic and geometry: "Vnde dicitur arismetrica et geometria. Arismetrica dicitur ab are[tes] quod est uirtus et rimos quod est numerus et thica [?] quod est sciencia quasi sciencia de uirtute numerj. Geometria dicitur a xeos quod est terra et metros quod est mensura quasi sciencia de mensura terre." (f. 248rb; f. 248v blank)

This manuscript, now housed in Catania, appears to have originated in Sicily. The scribe's name, Matheus de Collitortis de Castro Johannis, appears on f. 115v, where he identifies himself as a pupil of Jacobus Barbo, employed in the Chapel of Alfonso I, King of Naples.[63] The manuscript contains a treatise on counterpoint *secundum usum Regni Sicilie* (ff. 40v–41v), which further underscores its Sicilian origins. The date December 15, 1473 appears on f. 242v and is corroborated by the use of void notation.

The Catania manuscript is one of the three originating from the 1470s (Catania, Faenza, and Washington) and is also the poorest. Its use of void notation is especially reprehensible in the *Tractatus figurarum* where essential rhythmic differences are denoted by filled, void, semi-void, and red *figurae*. The notation has been quickly jotted down, as most of the manuscript appears to have been, with little concern for accuracy. The *Tractatus figurarum* appears conjoined with a section entitled *Quid sit prolacio*, thus explaining its omission in previous descriptions of this manuscript's contents.

Ch

Chicago, Newberry Library, Ms. 54.1[64]

Parchment; 59 folios, 25x18 cm
Pavia; 1391

1. The manuscript is lacking its first leaves; it begins in chapter 2 of Petrus de Sancto Dionysio's reworking of de Muris's *Notitia*. *Inc.* "[Chart of interval species from chapter 2] Capitulum 3 de invencione musice ..." *Exp.* "Explicite explicite quod erat implicite." (de Muris, *Notitia* [ed. Michels]) (ff. 1r–6v)
Colophon:
"Fons atrox eria pedalis truncus usya
Primi dant nomen bine factoris et omen
Papie 2. scriptum octobris 1391 per Fratrem G. de Anglia"
2. *Inc.* "Contrapunctum Magistri Phillipoti Andree artis nove ..." *Exp.* "... Et post quintam sexta erit, si fa mi re fuerit." (CS, 3:116–18) (ff. 6v–7r)

---

[63]*Lucidarium* (ed. Herlinger), p. 32.
[64]This description based upon de Muris, *Notitia* (ed. Michels), pp. 12–14.

3. *Tractatus figurarum. Inc.* "Tractatus Magistri Phillipoti Andree artis nove. Capitulum primum. Quoniam sicut Deo ..." *Exp.* "... Et si quatuor ascenderint usque octo numerus sic deficeret. Sic itaque ad complementum huius temporis consequtus sum. ideo refero gratias Deo. Amen." (ff. 7v–9r)

4. Diagram. (Triangle of Torkesey, see *Ms. Oxford, Bodley 842 [Willelmus] Breviarium regulare musicae*, ed. Gilbert Reaney; *Ms. British Muse[u]m, Royal 12.C.VI Tractatus de figuris sive de notis*, ed. Gilbert Reaney; Johannes Torkesey, *Declaratio Trianguli et Scuti*, ed. André Gilles and Gilbert Reaney, Corpus scriptorum de musica, no. 12 [n.p.: American Institute of Musicology, 1966]) (f. 9r)

5. Magister Albertus, table of proportions. *Inc.* "Sciendum est quod in superiori linea huius tabule ..." *Exp.* "... Tabula magistri Alberti super proportionibus." (f. 9v)

6. Music. Senleches, *La Harpe de Melodie*. (f. 10r)

7. Marchetto, *Lucidarium. Inc.* "Prohemium de epistola. Magnifico militi et potenti ..." *Exp.* "... Explicit Lucidarium Marcheti de Padua in arte musice plane et mensurate, inchoatum Cesene, Veroneque perfectum." (*Lucidarium* [ed. Herlinger]) (ff. 10v–33r)

8. Marchetto, *Pomerium. Inc.* "Incipit Pomerium Marcheti de Padua in arte musice ..." *Exp.* "... tempus musicum superius diffinitum est, primum quia." (Marchetto, *Pomerium*, ed. Giuseppe Vecchi, Corpus scriptorum de musica, no. 6 [n.p.: American Institute of Musicology, 1961]) (ff. 33r–42r; f. 42v blank)

9. Johannes de Muris, *Libellus de cantus mensurabilis. Inc.* "Tractatus venerabilis Magistri Johannis de Muris. Quilicet in arte practica ..." *Exp.* "... sufficiant in arte practica mensurabilis cantus anhelantibus introduci. Explicit musica venerati magistri Johannis de Muris." (CS, 3:46a–58b) (ff. 43r–49v)

10. Rules on counterpoint. *Inc.* "Hec sunt regule contrapuncti ..." *Exp.* "... ut fa. que est dyatessaron." (ff. 49r–50r)

11. Various alphabets (Hebrew, Greek, etc.) (ff. 50v–52v)

12. Anonymous, *Ars perfecta in musica Magistri Philippoti de Vitriaco. Inc.* "Incipiunt optime regule contrapuncti ..." *Exp.* "... Explicit ars perfecta in Musica Magistri Philippoti de Vitriaco." (CS, 3:28a–35b) (ff. 52v–56v; f. 57r blank)

13. Some annotations on mensuration. *Inc.* "Sicut se habent brevis et longa in modo perfecto ..." *Exp.* "... denotando et postea commixta significare." (ff. 57v–58v)

14. Examples of arabic numerals (f. 58v; f. 59r–v blank)

This beautiful manuscript is the Codex Vindobonensis, a copy of which (made by Ferdinandus Wolf around 1856) was viewed by Coussemaker.[65] The codex itself appeared on the rare book market in the twentieth century and was purchased by the Newberry Library from C. M. Nebehay in 1955.[66] It has been copied throughout in the same hand with the initials of most of the treatises illuminated in red and blue ink.[67] In the colophon to the first treatise, we find the statement "Papiae 2. scriptum octobris 1391 per Fratrem G. de Anglia."[68] The English influence is further attested by the inclusion of the Triangle of Torkesey (f. 9r), a diagram of rhythmic values very popular in England from the late fourteenth to the sixteenth centuries.[69]

As a source for the *Tractatus figurarum*, the importance of this manuscript cannot be overemphasized. Chronologically, it is the earliest of the *Tractatus*'s sources, as well as the most lavish. The care apparent in the physical copying of the text is also reflected in its accuracy. Much attention has been given to the transmission of the notation, with filled, void, semi-void, and red *figurae* appearing where described in the text. The occasional errors in the notation can perhaps be explained by a poor exemplar, for the manuscript's transmission of the notationally complex *Harpe de Melodie* of Senleches is quite accurate. The *Tractatus figurarum* is here ascribed to Phillipoctus Andrea, a claim not appearing elsewhere and whose veracity cannot be corroborated.

---

[65]CS, 3:xv.

[66]John W. Ohl, "Recent Additions to the Music Collection," *The Newberry Library Bulletin* 4 (1957): 192.

[67]At this time, I would like to take the opportunity to thank the Newberry Library for the short-term fellowship made available to me in order to study this manuscript.

[68]See f. 6v. This colophon also contains the cryptic phrase *Fons atrox eria pedalis truncus usya Primi dant nomen bine factoris et omen*. Following the instructions of the second phrase to take the first letters of the words of the first phrase in pairs to reveal the author, we expose Frater Petrus. In order for this to be correct, however, we must assume the scribe mistakenly wrote *fons* for *frons*, otherwise the first word would be *foater* instead of *frater*. The assumption seems justifiable in light of the result. And indeed, in other copies of this treatise, it is ascribed to Petrus de Sancto Dionysio.

[69]*Ms. Oxford, Bodley 842* ... Torkesey, *Declaratio*, p. 9.

Fa

Faenza, Biblioteca Comunale, Ms. 1117[70]

Paper; 98 folios, 25x18 cm
Italy; 1473–1474

(f. 1r–v blank)
1. Music (ff. 2r–11v; f. 12r–v blank)
2. Johannes de Muris, *Libellus cantus mensurabilis. Inc.* "Quilibet in arte practica ..." *Exp.* "... in arte practica mensurabilis cantus anhelantibus ac volentibus introduci. Et sic est finis." (CS, 3:46–58) (ff. 13r–15v)
3. *Tractatus figurarum. Inc.* "Incipit tractatus philippi de Caserta de diversis figuris per quas diversimode discantatur per aliquas regulas non sequentes modum tenoris sed alterius temporis. Quoniam sicut domino placuit ..." *Exp.* "... et sic quattuor ascendetur usque ad octo et numerus sic deficeret." Additional section on *traynour. Inc.* "Nunc videndum est qualiter ipsas ordinabimus ad discantandum diuersimode ..." *Exp.* "... In primo de tempore perfecto maiorum ponuntur pro duobus temporibus nouem semibreues rubee uel vacue ut hic [examples] Et sic est finis totius libri." (ff. 15v–17r)
4. Johannes de Muris, *Ars contrapuncti. Inc.* "Incipit liber artis contrapunctus secundum Johannem de muris ..." *Exp.* "... et ecce exempla omnium dictorum." (CS, 3:59–68) (ff. 17r–18r)
5. *Inc.* "Sequitur de tertio membro huius artis ..." *Exp.* "... la quinta, fa tertia, re unisonus." (f. 18v)
6. *Inc.* "Incipiunt regule artis cantus plani secundum magistrum Johannem de muris ..." *Exp.* "... septimi et octavi in acuto. Et sic est finis per me fratrem Johannem bonadies in conventu mantue 1473 4 octobris hora 15." (ff. 18v–20r)
7. Music (ff. 20v–21r)
8. *Inc.* "Nota quod 9 sunt species in arte contrapunctus ..." *Exp.* "... sed tamen nota quod non utimur talibus signis." (f. 21v)
9. Johannes Ciconia, *Tractatus de proportionibus. Inc.* "Venerabili viro et egregio domino Johanni gasparo ..." *Exp.* "... Et sic finis totius musice operis de proportionibus Johannis ciconiis canonici padue per me fratrem Jo. bo. 1473 20 novembris." (ff. 21v–23v)
10. *Inc.* "Gaudent brevitate moderni ..." *Exp.* "... quintus modus constat ex omnibus brevibus et semibrevibus, ut hic supra. Et sic finis per me fratrem Jo. bo. deo dante in conventu regii 1474 17 septembris, scilicet

---

[70]Description based upon Johannes Hothby, *De arte contrapuncti*, ed. Gilbert Reaney, Corpus scriptorum de musica, no. 26 (n.p.: American Institute of Musicology, 1977), pp. 97–100.

in die sancti lamberti post officium ante prandium tempore prioratus fratris luchini de lanfranchinis." (*Compendium musicae mensurabilis artis antiquae*, ed. F. Alberto Gallo, Corpus scriptorum de musica, no. 15 [n.p.: American Institute of Musicology, 1971]) (ff. 24r–25r)

11. Johannes Hothby, *De proportionibus. Inc.* "Regule fratris Jo. hothbi ..." *Exp.* "... ita iste infinite diminuuntur. Deo gratias." (CS, 3:328–30) (ff. 25v–26r)

12. Johannes Hothby, *De cantu figurato. Inc.* "De cantu figurato secundum eundem fratrem Jo. hothbi carmelitam ..." *Exp.* "... cum perfectione et sine perfectione. Amen. Et sic est finis per me fratrem Jo. bonadies in conventu regii hora primi noctis 1474 die 20a septembris." (CS, 3: 330–32) (f. 26r–v)

13. Johannes Hothby, *Nomina intervallorum. Inc.* "In genere enarmonico dyesis alcior ..." *Exp.* "... penthacordum bassioris." (f. 26v; f. 27r blank)

14. Music (ff. 27v–31r)

15. Jacobus de Regio, *Tractatus de proportionibus. Inc.* "Jacobus de Regio charmelita. Pro proportionum notitiam ..." *Exp.* "... Et sic finis ad laudem dei per me fratrem Jo. bonadies in conventu regii post vespras 1474 14 septembris." (ff. 31v–32r; ff. 32v–33v blank)

16. Johannes Hothby, *Regule hothbi supra contrapuntum. Inc.* "Quamvis species sive consonantie ..." *Exp.* "... retro numerando consonantis inveniemus. Et sic finis." (Hothby, *De arte contrapuncti* [ed. Reaney]) (f. 34r)

17. Nicasius Weyts, *Regule de cantu figurato. Inc.* "Regule nycasii weyts carmelite. Omnis nota in cantu mensurato ..." *Exp.* "... et ideo est duplex, ut dictum est." (CS, 3:262–64) (ff. 34v–35r)

18. *Inc.* "Presbiter bartholomeus Hothbista medicinus carmelita. Manus in dyatonico genere divisa ..." *Exp.* "... in cromatico genere pulcherrima habebit." (f. 35v)

19. Music (ff. 36r–60r)

20. Table of the tones. *Inc.* "Quantum ad tonos ..." *Exp.* "... constituunt tonum in figuris istis." (f. 60v)

21. Table of interval species. *Inc.* "Quantum ad diesis ..." *Exp.* "... et sic de singulis." (f. 61r; f. 61v blank)

22. *Inc.* "Regule fratris Jo. hothbi de monocordo manuali ..." *Exp.* "... hec septies quia septem sunt canne, etc." (f. 62r)

23. Table of mensurable music signs. "Hec sunt signa secundum J. Hothby" (f. 62v)

24. Music (ff. 63r–97v)

25. Notation examples in a sixteenth-century hand (f. 98r; f. 98v blank)

This manuscript was the product of Frater Bonadies, a student of Hothby in Lucca and one of the teachers of Franchinus Gaffurius.[71] His wide-ranging interest in music theory is reflected in the variety of treatises he copied. The date 1473 on f. 20r and 1474 on f. 32r gives an approximate range for the copying of the treatises contained in this manuscript. Bonadies apparently copied these *tractatus* for his own use, giving little thought to their legibility to anyone else.

The version of the *Tractatus figurarum* preserved in Faenza is quite accurate, undoubtedly reflected by Bonadies' expertise in music theory. Obvious care was taken with the notation, which for the most part is quite accurate.

Lo

London, British Library, Additional 4909[72]

Paper; 106 folios, 38.4x24.4 cm
England; early 18th century

1. Robertus de Handlo, *Regule. Inc.* "Incipiunt regulae cum Maximis Magistri Franconis cum additionibus aliorum musicorum compilatae a Roberto de Handlo. Gaudent brevitate moderni ..." *Exp.* "... Expliciunt regulae cum additionibus, finitae die Veneris proximo ante Pentecost anno Domini millesimo tricentesimo vicesimo sexto et caetera. Amen." (CS, 1:383–403) (ff. 1r–11r)
2. *Tractatus figurarum. Inc.* "Alius tractatulus de musica incerto authore. Incipit tractatus diversarum figurarum per quas dulces modi discantantur et ideo sequendo ordinem tenoris scilicet alterius temporis secundum Magistrum Egidium de Muris vel de Morino. Qui ut Deo placuit ..." *Exp.* "... et si quatuor ascenderent usque octo et unus sic deficeretis. Sic itaque ad completionem hujus operis concecutus sum, et ideo refero gratias Deo. Amen." Additional section on *traynour. Inc.* "Superius dictum est de diminutione et augmentatione figurarum, nunc videndum est ..." *Exp.* "... de tempore perfecto majori, de tempore perfecto minori, de tempore imperfecto majori [examples] de tempore imperfecto minori & de semibrevibus perfectis primo, accipo tenorem acutus antiphone ... si majores subtilitates habere volueris quam in isto volumine continentur, tunc studio fortior in Musica, et forte Deus dabit

---

[71]Seay, "Hothby," p. 729.

[72]This description with few modifications is based upon Peter Lefferts's forthcoming edition of Handlo in this series.

tibi per suam gratiam majorem intellectum atque subtilitatem."[73] (ff. 11v–17v)

3. *Inc.* "Alius tractatulus de musica, incerto authore. Pro aliqui notitia de musica de musica habenda ..." *Exp.* "... vide Orphei et Amphionis modulationes, ac alias musicae virtutes quas ponit Macrobius de sompno Scipionis, libro 2do. Ex hiis omnibus praecedentibus colligo hanc divisionem sequentem: [example]." (ff. 17v–20r)

4. *Inc.* "Secundo. Principaliter videndum est, primo, de arte musicae ac elementorum sive literarum quae claves vocantur inventione ..." *Exp.* "... sesquetertius est tunc sequitur quinarius numerus minor est quaternario et quaternarius ternario et ternarius numerus binario et binarius numerus minor est unitate et sic sequitur quod in majoribus numeris minor est proportio et in minoribus numeris minor proportio continentur." (ff. 20v–26v)

5. *Inc.* "In superioribus particulis dictum est de divisione musicae, de ejus etiam inventione ac de proportionibus ad monocordi divisionem pertinentibus, in ista parte declarandum est de plano cantu qui in quinque consistit. Prima est ..." *Exp.* "... ex praedictis vero tredecim speciebus nulla in numerorum musicalium proportione recipitur praeter tonum quae est in sesqueoctava proportione, et dyatessaron quae est in sesquetertia proportione, et diapente quae est in sesquealtera proportione et diapason quae semper duplam proportionem, ut superius in secundo principali capitulo et cetera." (ff. 26v–31r)

6. Diagram of a triangle. *Inc.* "1a. Omnis nota praeter simplam carent puncto omnino imperfecta est ..." *Exp.* "... omnis nota quae post se punctum habet omnino perfecta dicitur, quia et ipsa perfecta est, et omnes partes ipsam oblique componentes omnino perfecte sunt excepta sola simpla quae est inpartibilis." (ff. 31r–31v)

7. *Inc.* "Dictis aliquibus circa planum cantum, restat aliud dicendum de cantu sive musica mensurabili, circa quod primo dicendum est de qualitate musicae mensurabilis, secundo de divisione ..." *Exp.* "... et haec de musicae continuae et etiam discretae principiis sufficiant ad praesens, que tanto ut credo acceptiora sunt quanto aliorum dictis concordiam habent nam in isto libello nichil apposui quod non ab auctoritatibus et a magistris peritis et approbatis mediante gratia Dei addici. Explicit." (ff. 31v–56r)

8. *Inc.* "Cognita modulatione melorum secundum vaim octo troporum et secundum usum consuetudinem fidei catholicae ..." *Exp.* "... in nomine et honore sanctissimi mediatoris omnium, qui est verus salvator, Jesus Christus, filius dei vivi, et qui est corona et gloria omnium sanctorum ad quam gloriam possumus omnes pervenire cum sanctissimo." (CS, 1:327a–364b) (ff. 56v–93r)

---

[73]In this codex, the *Tractatus figurarum* and *De modo componendi* have been conjoined.

9. *Inc.* "Sequitur de sinemenis sic ..." *Exp.* "... omnis spiritus laudet Dominum etc. cuncta bona etc. Explicit." (Prosdocimo de' Beldomandi, *Brevis summula* [ed. Herlinger], pp. 123–35) (ff. 93r–94v)

10. *Inc.* "Est autem unisonus ..." *Exp.* "... Item si descendat per diatessaron sta in eodem." (CS, 1:364a–65b) (ff. 94v–96r)

11. Guidonian hand and musical notation. (ff. 96v–97v)

12. *Inc.* "Cum in isto tractatu de figuris sive de notis quae sunt ..." *Exp.* "... et sic finitur capitulum tertium etc." (CS, 1:369a–77b) (ff. 98r–104v)

13. *Faus semblaunt* [French rondeau a 2]. (Johannes Wolf, *Geschichte der Mensural-Notation von 1250–1460*, 3 vols. [Leipzig: Breitkopf und Härtel, 1904], 2:15–16 and 3: 27–28) (f. 104v)

14. Walter Odington, *De speculatione musicae* [3 excerpts]. (Walter Odington, *Summa de speculatione musicae,* ed. Frederick F. Hammond, Corpus scriptorum de musicae, no. 14 [n.p.: American Institute of Musicology, 1970]).

a. *Inc.* "Notum quod est unum genus organici ..." *Exp.* "... et hujusmodi cantus truncatus dicitur a rei convenientia qui et hoequets dicitur — haec Odyngton."

b. *Inc.* "Longa perficitur cum longa praecedit ..." *Exp.* "... vel valor brevis resolute in semibreves sic [example]."

c. *Inc.* "De modis quibus procedunt cantus organici. Modus in hac parte est ..." *Exp.* "... Primus itaque secundi imperfectus."

This manuscript, now in the British Library, is a transcript of the musical sections of Tiberius B.IX, made by Johann Christoph Pepusch before the disastrous fire of 1731 in the Cotton Library.[74] Little is known of the original from which Pepusch copied, but Arlt dates the remaining fragments to the late fourteenth century, thus establishing its importance.[75] The Pepusch copy is in excellent shape and can be read with ease.

As a source for the *Tractatus figurarum*, granted the chronological importance of its tradition, the Pepusch manuscript is of limited interest. The text is good for the most part, with the exception of some curious words (e.g., *dulces modi* for *diversimode*), which appear to be unusual expansions by Pepusch of abbreviations in the text he was copying. The notation becomes quite cursory, a misfortune augmented by the fact that this is one of the few sources to include an enlarged set of examples following the *Tractatus*. The true importance of this manuscript lies in its conveyance of the early tradition

---

[74]Augustus Hughes-Hughes, *Catalogue of Manuscript Music in the British Museum*, 3 vols. (London: British Museum, 1909), 3:303.

[75]Arlt, p. 38.

ascribing the *Tractatus figurarum* to Egidius.[76] It also lends weight to the inclusion of the final section on *trayn* or *traynour* as an original part of the treatise.

Mi

Milano, Biblioteca Ambrosiana, Ms. I 20 inf.[77]

Paper; 44 folios, 28x19 cm
Northern Italy; after 1440

1. *Inc.* "Incipit palma choralis de rationibus cantus ecclexiastici edita a Magistro Johanne de olomons. Alias de Casteliono Scolastico ..." *Exp.* "... quem de olomons profers flamen tuus ille Johannes. Finis. Explicit palma choralis." (Johannes de Olomons, *Palma Choralis*, Colorado College Music Press Critical Texts, no. 6 [Colorado Springs: Colorado College Music Press, 1977]) (ff. 1r–24v)
2. Collection of extracts from musical treatises.

   a. *Inc.* "Ratio sequitus est ista. Si aliquis vult scire sequitum ..." *Exp.* "... et hoc non moveatur." (*De organo mediolanensi*, in Jacques Handschin, "Aus der alten Musiktheorie," *Acta Musicologica* 15 [1943]: 5–6) (f. 25r)

   b. *De modis sive tonis. Inc.* "Octo sunt toni quorum primus et secundus ..." *Exp.* "... sexto et octavo per tertiam vocem infra." (f. 25r–v)

   c. Franco de Colonia, *Compendium musicae mensurabilis. Inc.* "[G]audent brevitate moderni: quandocumque punctus quadrus ..." *Exp.* "... quinto modo procedit hec mensura ex omnibus brevibus et semibrevibus et requiritur iste modus naturaliter pausa unius temporis ut hic." (ff. 25v–27v)

   d. *Inc.* "Ratio contrapuncti est ista. Qui vult scire contrapunctum ..." *Exp.* "... et est dissonantia tam in ascendendo quam in descendendo." (ff. 27v–28r)

   e. *Inc.* "Ratio contraponti. In gamaut possunt fieri tres voces ..." *Exp.* "... la unisonus, fa tertia, re quinta, ut sexta." (ff. 28r–v)
3. Johannes Hothby, *Tractatus de arte contrapuncti* [lacking the end; on f. 29r the Latin changes to Italian]. *Inc.* "In primo dico quod contrapunctum requirit habere quatuor res ..." *Exp.* "... nel terzo grado, zoe grado de quinta, ut a doe consonanze e doe dissonanze, zoe quinta,

---

[76]"Incipit tractatus diversarum figurarum ... secundum Magistrum Egidium de Muris vel de Morino" (see section 2).

[77]Based on the description in Hothby, *De arte contrapuncti* (ed. Reaney), pp. 22–23.

viii, vi, x; quinta che dice ut, viii che dice fa, vi che dice re, x che dice la re." (Hothby, *De arte contrapuncti* [ed. Reaney], pp. 15–49) (ff. 28v–30v)

4. Johannes de Muris, *Libellus cantus mensurabilis*. *Inc.* "Johannes de Muris. Adsit principio Virga maria meo. Quilibet in arte pratica mensurabilis cantus erudiri mediocriter effectans ..." *Exp.* "... et predicta quamvis rudia sufficiant in artem praticam mensurabilis cantus anelantibus introdici." (CS, 3:46–58) (ff. 31r–34v)

5. *Tractatus figurarum*. *Inc.* "Incipit tractatus figurarum per quas diversimode discantatur non sequentes ordinem tenoris sed alterius temporis. Quoniam sicut deo placuit ..." *Exp.* "... et si quatuor ascenderet usque ad octo et numeraueritis sic deficeret sic itaque ad complementum huius operis consecutus sum. Deo refero gratias." Additional section on *traynour*. *Inc.* "Nunc dicendum est qualiter ipsas ordinabimus ad discantandum diuersimode ..." *Exp.* "... In primo de tempore perfecto maiori ponitur pro duobus temporibus nouem semibreues uacuas ut hic" [lacking examples]. (ff. 34v–36r)

6. Philippotus Andrea, *Regulae contrapuncti*. *Inc.* "Post octavam quintam si note tendunt ..." *Exp.* "... post sextam octavam si cantus descendit per unum. Et sic est finis. Deo gratias. Amen." (CS, 3:116–18) (f. 36r–v)

7. Marchetto, *Lucidarium* [lacking the end]. *Inc.* "Epistola Marcheti de padua domino Raynerio. Magnifico militi et potenti domino suo ..." *Exp.* "... habemus ergo ex dictis quod cum sumus ad novenarium divisionem." (*Lucidarium* [ed. Herlinger]) (ff. 36v–39r; ff. 39v–40r blank)

8. *Inc.* "Primus tonus sic incipit ..." *Exp.* "... benedicamus domi[n]o. Deo dicamus gratias." (ff. 41r–43r; ff. 43v–44v blank)

The correct dating of this manuscript is confused by the appearance of the date 1405 on f. 1r. It has been written in a hand other than that of the manuscript itself and has been repeated in a prefatory sheet that Albert Seay believed to have been added by a librarian at a later date, accepting the date as correct.[78] Herlinger correctly points out a reference in the dedication of the *Palma Choralis* to Cardinal Branda of Piacenza, Bishop of Sabina, who was named Bishop in 1440 and who died in 1443, thus giving *termini post et ante quem* for the copying of the manuscript.[79] It has been suggested that the Milan manuscript was in part copied from the Washington.[80] The stemma, however, will show these two coming from widely varying traditions, and so

---

[78] Johannes de Olomons, *Palma choralis*, p. i.

[79] *Lucidarium* (ed. Herlinger), p. 48.

[80] Hothby, *De arte contrapuncti* (ed. Reaney), p. 10.

the suggestion seems dubious. The myriad Italianate spellings and the inclusion of the *Palma Choralis* of Johannes Olomons suggest a northern Italian, if not a Milanese origin.[81]

The copy of the *Tractatus figurarum* included in this codex is moderately corrupt. Equally lamentable is the omission of notation, for only one example is included: that of the hollow dot. The concept must have been so foreign to the copyist that he could not help but include it.

Na

Napoli, Biblioteca Nazionale, Ms. VIII D 12[82]

Paper; 27 folios (3rd section), 21x16 cm
Italy; 15th century

1. Section concerning the modes.
    a. *Inc.* "Nota quod octo sunt toni cantus ..." *Exp.* "... Op tenet ut fa. Et hec de tonis presens dicta sufficiant." (CS, 3:99a–100b) (ff. 33r–35v)
    b. Formulas for the various tones (f. 36r)
    c. *Inc.* "Primus cum sexto ..." *Exp.* "... semper bene recordor." (f. 37r)
2. *Inc.* "Sequitur de primo contrapuncto. Nota quod contrapunctus est fundamentum ..." *Exp.* "... et sic finitur primus contrapunctus. Et hec de primo contrapuncto presens dicta" [for the discussion of the second and third types of counterpoint, see below ff. 56r–57r]. (ff. 37r–38r)
3. *Inc.* "Q[?]ecipe lo pepe trito et tengalo ..." *Exp.* "... la bona vox." (f. 38v)
4. "Incipit [illegible] regularum ..." (f. 39r; f. 39v blank)
5. Johannes de Muris, *Libellus cantus mensurabilis*. *Inc.* "Quilibet in arte praticha mensurabilis cantus ..." *Exp.* "... anellantibus introducy." (CS, 3:46–58) (ff. 40r–45v)
6. *Tractatus figurarum*. *Inc.* "Incipit tractatus figurarum per quas diversimode discantantur per aliquas non sequentes modum tenoris set alterius temporibus. Quoniam sicut domino placuit ..." *Exp.* "... et si quatuor ascendentur vsque ad octo et numerus sic defyceret sic itaque ad com-

---

[81]*Lucidarium* (ed. Herlinger), p. 47.

[82]Description based upon Pieter Fischer, ed., *The Theory of Music from the Carolingian Era up to 1400*, Répertoire international des sources musicales, BIII/2 (München-Duisburg: G. Henle, 1968), pp. 70–72. In the future, this note will be abbreviated as RISM BIII/2.

plementum vius hoperis consecutus sum, ideo deo gratias refero." Additional section on *traynour. Inc.* "Nunc videndum est qualiter ipsas ordinabimus ad discantandum sic diuersimode ..." *Exp.* "... in primo de tempore perfecto maiori ponitur pro duobus temporibus nouem semibreves vacue vel rubee ut hic apparet inferius per exemplum [examples]." (ff. 45v–48r)

7. Johannes de Muris, *Ars contrapuncti. Inc.* "Quilibet apfectans scire contrapunctum ..." *Exp.* "... vide et quere diminutionem eius." (CS, 3:59–68a, nota) (ff. 48r–51v)
8. *Inc.* "Sequitur de tertio membro ..." *Exp.* "... tibi gratiarum actio in secula seculorum amen" [for a discussion of the first type of counterpoint, see above ff. 37r–38r]. (f. 51v)
9. *Inc.* "Nota quod unisonus de ut est simile ut ..." *Exp.* "... duodecima est la etc." (ff. 51v–52r)
10. "Manus Boetii" [three hands pointing to three lists of solmization syllables]. (f. 52r)
11. *Inc.* "Musicha unde costa ex septem consonantiis ..." *Exp.* "... et hoc de causa perfectionis esse dicitur etc." (f. 52r–v)
12. "Horatio beata virgo dey ..." (f. 53r; f. 53v blank)
13. *Inc.* "Nota quod diatesseron est spatium quatuor vocum ..." *Exp.* "... et de proportionibus presens dicta supficient [eight hands pointing to the eight modes] Pri re la ... Op tenet ut fa." (f. 54r)
14. *Inc.* "Nota quod brevis perfecta ..." *Exp.* "... ad perficiendum massimas etc." (f. 54v)
15. *Inc.* "Filius [illegible] dey ..." *Exp.* "... Et prima lux bene." (f. 55r)
16. Chart "[ ]us numerus. Anno 1400 54 ..." (f. 55v)
17. *Inc.* "Nota quod secundus contrapunctus incipit in B grave ... Sequitur de tertio contrapuncto ..." *Exp.* "... ut sexta de sopto." (ff. 56r–57r; 57v–59r blank)

This codex is a collection of three separate manuscripts that have been bound together. The first section comprises ff. 1–22 and comes from the twelfth century; the second, ff. 23–32, from the thirteenth; and the last, ff. 33–59, from the fifteenth.[83] The third section is written in a clear, fifteenth-century hand exhibiting many typical Italianate variants (*duples, homnibus, instrusserunt*). Aside from these orthographical peculiarities, the text is quite good, and the notation is carefully preserved as well. No major break is made between the *Tractatus figurarum* and the treatise that precedes it.

---

[83]Raffaele Arnese, *I Codici notati della Biblioteca Nazionale di Napoli*, Biblioteca di bibliografia italiana, no. 47 (Firenze: Leo S. Olschki, 1967), p. 161.

Pi

Pisa, Biblioteca Universitaria, Ms. 606 II[84]

Paper; 58 pages, 27x20 cm
North-east of Italy; after 1411

1. Johannes de Muris, *Musica speculativa*. *Inc.* "Quoniam musica est de numero relato ad sonos ..." *Exp.* "... quorum figure sunt in hoc ordine consequentes. Explicit musica magistri Johannis de Muris." (*Scriptores ecclesiastici de musica sacra potissimum* [henceforward: GS], 3 vols., ed. Martin Gerbert [St. Blaise: Typis San-Blasianis, 1784; reprint ed., Hildesheim: Olms, 1963], 3:256–83) (pp. 1–18)
2. Johannes de Muris, *Libellus cantus mensurabilis*. *Inc.* "Quilibet in arte pratica mensurabilis cantus erudiri mediocriter ..." *Exp.* "... et predicta quamvis rudia sufficiant in arte pratica mensurabilis cantus anellantibus introduci. Deo gratias." (CS, 3:46–58) (pp. 19–29)
3. *Tractatus figurarum*. *Inc.* "Incipit tractatus figurarum per quas diversimode discantatur per aliquas non sequentes modum tenoris sed alterius temporis. Quoniam sicut domino placuit ..." *Exp.* "... Et si quatuor ascendetur ascendatur usque ad octo et numerus sic deficet. Sic itaque ad complementum huius operis consecutus sum. deo deo gratias refferro." Additional section on *traynour*. *Inc.* "Nunc videndum est qualiter ipsas ordinabimus ad discantandum diuersimode ..." *Exp.* "... In primo de tempore perfecto maiori ponuntur pro duobus temporibus nouem semibreues uacue ut hic rubee [examples]." (pp. 30–33)
4. Johannes de Muris, *Ars contrapuncti*. *Inc.* "Ars contrapuncti Johannis de Muris. Quilibet affectans scire contrapunctum ..." *Exp.* "... et de conclusionibus contrapuncti quantum ad omnia tempora hec sufficiant. Videlicet quibus cantores utuntur Ternario et Binario ... Vide quere diminutiones ipsius." (CS, 3:59–68) [There follows a solmization table with the rubricated title "Manus Boecii"] (pp. 34–42)
5. *Inc.* "Sequitur de Tertio membro huius artis ..." *Exp.* "... tibi gratiarum actio in secula seculorum. Amen." (p. 43)
6. Johannes de Ciconia, *Liber de proportionibus* (1411). (pp. 44–51)
7. A compendium of the *Ars contrapuncti* of Johannes de Garlandia. *Inc.* "Volentibus introduci in arte contrapuncti ..." *Exp.* "... et moderni semper adiungunt alteras species 15as sive duplicem 8as. Et hec dicta de contrapuncti sufficiant in nostra schola musicali." (CS, 3:12–13) (p. 51)
8. *Inc.* "Quoniam de canendi scientia doctrinam sumus facturi ..." *Exp.* "... terminatur enim in eisdem litteris in quibus" [mutilated at the end].

---

[84]RISM BIII/2, pp. 81–84, where only the second part is described.

(Albert Seay, "An Anonymous Treatise from St. Martial," *Annales musicologiques* 5 [1957]: 13–36) (pp. 52–57)

9. A sixteenth-century hand has written at the head "Jusquini." *Inc.* "Nota quod novem sunt consonantie ..." *Exp.* "... fit tam in ascensu quam descensu." (CS, 3:12–13) (p. 58)

The Pisa codex is composed of two large parts. The *explicit* to Ciconia's *Liber de proportionibus* contained in the second part described above (section 6) reads: "explicit liber de proportionibus musicae Johannis de Ciconiis paduani in orbe famosissimi Musici anno Domini MCCCCXI"; and so gives a date after which the treatises in this section must have been copied.[85] The Faenza and Pisa manuscripts occasionally share variants that suggest a close relationship. For instance, they are the only two manuscripts to label chapter 6 as chapter 3, and in chapter 6 (84.13), they both substitute the word *maiorum* for *minorum*. In the closing section on *traynour*, both share notational variants as well. Nevertheless, the many variants they do not share preclude a direct relationship and suggest instead that both derive from the same source, or that an intervening source exists. In the latter case, the dating of the manuscripts would imply that the Faenza codex was ultimately derived from the Pisa.

Ro1

Roma, Biblioteca Apostolica Vaticana, Palatinus lat. 1377[86]

Paper; 94 folios (first section), 29x20 cm
Italy; late 14th century

1. Table of contents. "Petri paduani tractatus in motu oct[?] sphere | Aristotilis liber de conductibus Aqvaris | Liber de presagiis tempestatium | Tadei liber de speculis | Iordani tractatus de ponderibus." (f. [i])
2. *Inc.* "Incipit tractatus quem composuit magister petrus paduanus in motu 8r spere ..." *Exp.* "... que est multorum [illegible]." (ff. 1r–5r)
3. *Inc.* "Incipit liber Aristotilis de conductibus aquarum ..." *Exp.* "... Explicit philosophus de aquarum conductibus." (ff. 5r–9r, 9v blank)
4. *Inc.* "Incipit liber de presagiis tempestatium ..." *Exp.* "... Explicit liber de presagiis tempestatium." (ff. 10r–11r)
5. *Inc.* "Incipit liber tadei de speculis ..." *Exp.* "... Explicit iste liber de speculis." (ff. 11v–18v)

---

[85]*Pomerium* (ed. Vecchi), p. 12.
[86]RISM BIII/2, pp. 110–11.

6. *Inc.* "Ire 2o perspectum [illegible] hec octo ..." *Exp.* "... Explicit tractatus Iordani de ponderibus cum comento." (ff. 18v–20v)
7. *Inc.* "Liber abiahe ducis ..." *Exp.* "... Tabula nouenaria." (ff. 21r–43v)
8. Chart. "Ante meridiem" (f. 44r)
9. Chart. "Post meridiem." Above the chart is written "Liber conuentus S. Anastasie ..." (f. 44v)
10. *Inc.* "Sequitur regula ..." (f. 45r)
11. Mathematical tables. "Incipit libellus arismetrice" (f. 45v)
12. Chart. "QVADRANS HOROLOGII HORIZONTALIS" (f. 46r)
13. Chart. "QVADRATVM HORARIVM GENERALE" (f. 46v)
14. *Inc.* "Incipit tractatus de numeris qui dicitur algorissmus ..." *Exp.* "... Explicit liber algo [illegible]." (ff. 47r–50v)
15. *Inc.* "Incipit tractatus de sphera magistri Johannis de sacroboscho ..." *Exp.* "... Explicit tractatus de spera magistri Johannis de Sacroboscho scripsit et [?] per me Jacobus de Barbo [?]." (ff. 51r–58r)
16. Tables of mathematical properties. (f. 59r-v)
17. Johannes de Muris, *Musica speculativa*. *Inc.* "Incipit ars speculativa Magistri Johannis de Muris Musici sapientissimi. Quoniam musica est de numero relato ad sonos ..." *Exp.* "... in hoc ordine consequentes. Explicit musica magistri Johannis de Muris, Musicorum sapientissimi." (GS, 3:256–83) (ff. 60r–81r)
18. Diagram of intervals. (f. 81v)
19. Johannes de Muris, *Libellus cantus mensurabilis*. *Inc.* "Incipit tractatus artis musice gallicane. Quilibet in arte plattica ..." *Exp.* "... anelantibus introduci." (CS, 3:46–58) (ff. 82r–89v)
20. *Tractatus figurarum. Inc.* "Incipit tractatus figurarum per quas diversimode discantatur per aliquos non sequentes modum tenorum sed alterius temporius. Quoniam sicut domino placuit ..." *Exp.* "... et si quatuor ascenderet usque ad octo et numerus sic deficeret. Sic itaque ad complementum huius operis assecutus sum. Ideo deo refero gracias." Additional section on *traynour. Inc.* "Nunc videndum est quomodo ordinabimus ipsas ad discantandum diuersimode ..." *Exp.* "... In primo de tempore perfecto maioris ponuntur pro duobus temporibus novem semibreves vacue ut hic apparet clare patet [without examples]." (ff. 89v–93v)
21. Johannes de Muris, *Ars contrapuncti* [first part]. *Inc.* "Ars contrapunctus Magistri Johannis de Muris summarie compilata hic inferius describitur. Quilibet affectans scire ..." *Exp.* "... discantus debet descendere et e converso. Et hec ad presens de contrapuncto dicta sufficiant. Explicit Tractatus contrapuncti secundum Magistrum Johannem de Muris." (CS, 3:59–60a) (ff. 93v–94v; f. 94[i.e., 95]a blank)

This codex is composed of two separate sections: the first (ff. 1–94) from the fourteenth century and the second (ff. 95–110) from the eleventh century. The manuscript's fourteenth-century origin is attested by the angularity of the script, the heavily shaded ascenders of the *f* and *s*, which drop below the line, and the uncial *d* pointed to the left. The text preserved is quite accurate and the examples moderately so. The lack of extensive abbreviations clarifies uncertain readings from other sources. It is curious that the manuscript includes the text of the addendum that treats *traynour* but does not include the examples.

Ro5

Roma, Biblioteca Apostolica Vaticana, lat. 5321[87]

Paper; 25 folios, 29x20 cm
Italy; late 14th to early 15th century

1. *Inc.* "[Q]uot sunt iuncture manus [?] Sunt decem et novem scilicet A. B. C. d ..." *Exp.* "... omnis autenticus habet suum subiugalem sub se etc. "(f. 1r; f. 1v blank)
2. Johannes de Muris, *Libellus cantus mensurabilis. Inc.* "Quilibet in arte pratica ..." *Exp.* "... quamvis rudia sufficiant in arte mensurabilis cantus anelantibus introduci. Explicit practica cantus mensurabilis secundum magistrum Johannem de Muris et cetera." (CS, 3:46–58) (ff. 2r–6r)
3. *Tractatus figurarum. Inc.* "Quoniam sicut domino placuit ..." *Exp.* "... Et sic quatuor ascenderent usque ad octo. et nunc sic deficerent. Sic itaque ad complementum huius operis consecutus sum ideo refero gratias deo." Additional section on *traynour. Inc.* "Superius dictum est de augmentatione atque diminucione figurarum nunc dicendum est qualiter ipsas ordinabis ..." *Exp.* "... Et primo de tempori perfecti maioris et ponuntur autem [illegible] nouem semibreues uacuas [illegible] [examples] Capitulum quartum de modo componendi tenores motettorum. Primo accipe tenorum ... et retro clausum. Deo Gratias. Explicit tractatus cantus mensurabilis secundum magistrum egidium de murino."[88] (*De modo componendi*, CS, 3:124–28) (ff. 6r–9v)
4. Prosdocimo de' Beldomandi, *Tractatus de contrapuncto. Inc.* "Incipit contrapunctus Magistri prosdocimi de beldemandis patavii. [S]cribit aristoteles ..." *Exp.* "... si ipsa subtiliter speculabitur. Sufficiant ergo ista ... Deo gratias Amen. Explicit contrapunctus prosdocimi de belde-

---

[87]RISM BIII/2, pp. 98–99.

[88]As in the London codex, the *Tractatus figurarum* is here conjoined with the *De modo componendi*.

mandis paduani in castro montagnano paduani districtus anno domini 1412 compilatus. Amen." (Prosdocimo de' Beldomandi, *Contrapunctus*, ed. Jan Herlinger, Greek and Latin Music Theory, vol. 1 [Lincoln: University of Nebraska Press, 1984]) (ff. 9v–11v)

5. Johannes de Muris, *Musica speculativa*. *Inc*. "Quoniam musica est de sono ..." *Exp*. "... remissum sit in e et g et ab a in e. croma in gravi parte repertum [diagram]." (GS, 3:256–77b) (ff. 12r–20r)

6. A treatise by Prosdocimo on numerical proportions. *Inc*. "[illegible] artem calculators ..." *Exp*. "... explicit canum in quo docetur modus hanc tabulam insia scriptum componendi ac peripam in omnibus specibus pratice arismetice operandi per prosdocimum de beldemando de padua compilatus deo gratias Amen" [A numerical chart follows]. (ff. 20r–22r; f. 22v blank)

7. [Philippe de Vitry?], *Ars contrapuncti*. *Inc*. "[V]olentibus introduci in arte contrapuncti ..." *Exp*. "... ut sepius dictum est. Et hec dicta de contrapuncto sive nota contra notam ad presens sufficiant. Explicit ars contrapunctus secundum philippum de vitriaco et cetera." (CS, 3:23–27) (ff. 23r–25va)

8. Johannes de Muris, *Summa artis contrapuncti*. *Inc*. "Ars contrapuncti Johannis de Muris summarie compilatus. Quilibet affectans scire contrapunctum ..." *Exp*. "... Item sciendum quod quando tenor ascendit cantus debet descendere et e converso. Explicit tract[atus?] Johannis de muris quoad artem contrapuncti." (CS, 3:59–60a) (25vb)

The manuscript's Italian provenance is revealed by its characteristic abbreviation for *qui* and the use of the uncrossed Tironian *et* sign. The use of the looped four and the uncial *d* with its ascender strongly pointed to the left are typical of the fourteenth century. The manuscript itself is suffering from ink rusting, making many readings problematic. The text and examples are fair, containing many variants peculiar to a group of four manuscripts (Lo, Ro5, Si, Wa), which will be discussed below in the section on the stemma. The *Tractatus figurarum* is united by continuous chapter references to the *De modo componendi* and is attributed to Egidius de Murino.

Se1-3

Sevilla, Catedral Metropolitana, Biblioteca Capitular y Colombina, 5.2.25[89]

Parchment and paper; 137 folios, 22x15 cm
Italy; mid 14th to early 15th century

1. *Inc.* "Ars musice mensurate secundum Guidonem. Ad habendam aliqualem noticiam figurarum simplicium et compositarum ..." *Exp.* "... a me indigno cantore extitit compilatum Deo reddatur laus et gloria per cuncta secula. Amen." (ff. 1r–5r)
2. Marchetto, *Lucidarium*. *Inc.* "Incipit lucidarium marcheti de padua in plana musica ..." *Exp.* "... et preconem iubet praticari. Et hec de musica plana sufficiant. Explicit lucidarium marchettji de Padua in arte musice ychoatum Cesene et perfectum Verone." (*Lucidarium* [ed. Herlinger]) (ff. 5r–20v)
3. Music (f. 22v)
4. *Inc.* "Tractatus de musica. Primo videamus quid sit musica et unde dicatur. Diffinitio. Musica est motus vocum qui fit per arsim et per tesim ..." *Exp.* "... stillum aplica. Explicit compendiolum sive excepta de musica optime per quendam dilligentissime compillata." (ff. 24r–36v)
5. *Inc.* "De modo organicandi. Omnis homo qui vult bene organicare ..." *Exp.* "... et octavam ascendere." (ff. 36v–27v)
6. *Inc.* "Omnis proportio vel est comuniter dicta vel proprie dicta ..." *Exp.* "... duple proporcionis sicut dyamatur ad costam." (f. 37v)
7. *Inc.* "Primus cum sexto .fa.sol.la. semper habeto ..." *Exp.* "... omnes esse recto dox (?)."(f. 38r)
8. Circular chart. (f. 38v; f. 39r–v blank [heavily damaged—scraped?])
9. Musical examples. *Inc.* "Semitonum est inperfectum sonum ..." *Exp.* "... dyapente in proportione emiolia id est sexquialtera." (f. 40r)
10. *Inc.* "Omnes gentes plaudite..." *Exp.* "... che compani [illegible]." (f. 40v)
11. *Inc.* "Cum boecius rome degeret ..." *Exp.* "... et sicut scriptum est omnis laus in fine cantus." (ff. 41r–48r)
12. Landini, *Fortuna ria*. (ff. 48v–49r)
13. *Inc.* "Primus cum sexto fa sol la semper habetur ..." *Exp.* "... sic omnibus esse recordor." (f. 49v)

---

[89]Description based on F. Alberto Gallo, "Alcune fonti poco note di musica teorica e pratica," in *Ars nova italiana del trecento: Convegni di studio 1961–1967* (Certaldo: Centro di studi sull'Ars Nova italiana del trecento, 1968), pp. 59–73.

14. *Inc.* "Introducendis in arte musice primo videndum est ..." *Exp.* "... acutis et superacutis litteris ut apparet hic." (ff. 50r–53r)
15. *Inc.* "Nota quod tres sunt modi cantandi ..." *Exp.* "... primus ad quintam." (ff. 56r–v)
16. Musical fragment. Tenor de monaco so tucto ziusu. (f. 57v)
17. "Benedicamus domino" [music]. (f. 58r)
18. *Inc.* "Sciendum est quod novem sunt species contrapuncti ..." *Exp.* "... nos debemus ascendere." (f. 58v)
19. Musical fragment. Contratenor de monaco so tucto ziusu. (f. 58v)
20. [Ballata for 2 voices] *Chi temp a per amore.* (f. 59r)
21. Musical fragment. (f. 59v)
22. *Inc.* "Incipit ars qualiter et quomodo debent fieri mottettj. in nomine domini amen. Moctetti debent fieri hoc modo. Primo accipe tenorem ..." *Exp.* "... et illa perfectio debet durare usque ad finem. Deo gratias Amen." (ff. 60r–62v)
23. *Inc.* "Omni desideranti notitiam artis mensurabilis tam nove quam veteris obtinere ..." *Exp.* "... super lineam est minime. Ut hic apparet. [example] Explicit de gratias referamus. Amen." (ff. 63r–64v)
24. *Inc.* "Iste sunt regule in discantu ..." *Exp.* "... super nota pro nota sicut in exemplis supradictis et infranotatis patet [musical examples]." (f. 65r–v)
25. *Inc.* "Ad brevem notitiam contrapuncti nota ..." *Exp.* "... in octava cum tenora." (f. 66r)
26. *Inc.* "Regula ad faciendum ballatam Rondellum et virondellum ut sequitur. In primis quomodo debet fieri ballata ..." *Exp.* "... et retro habet clausum. Deo gratias. Amen." (f. 66r)
27. *Inc.* "Incipit ars Magistri Marchectj de Padua super cantum planum. Sciendum est quod aniquitus ..." *Exp.* "... Et hoc quo ad tonorum cognitionem. Predicta sunt Magistri Marcj de Padua expertissimi doctoris musice. et secundum eum predicta compilavj." (ff. 66v–68v)
28. *Inc.* "Primus ad tertiam ..." *Exp.* "... octauus in eodem loco dicendo ut|relut. et cetera."(f. 68v)
29. *Inc.* "Adsit principio virgo maria meo quilibet in arte pratica mensurabilis cantus erudiri mediocriter affectans ..." *Exp.* "... non servatur motetis. Exempla patent in motetis. Et predicta quamvis rudia sufficiant in arte pratica mensurabilis cantu volentibus introduci." (ff. 70r–76r)
30. *Inc.* "Sequitur de proposicionibus. [P]roposicio est quidam habitudo duorum terminorum adinvicem ..." *Exp.* "... bis diapason in quadrupla. Ex hec de proporcionibus ad presens dicta sufficient. Deo gracias. Amen." (ff. 76v–77v)
31. *Inc.* "[A]d habendum discantum artis musice. Primo videndum est quid sit discantus et unde dicatur. Discantus est ..." *Exp.* "... secundum ascensum et descensum planj cantus." (ff. 78r–79r)

32. *Inc.* "Septem sunt species discantus ..." *Exp.* "... in inperfectis speciebus discantus." (ff. 79r–80r)
33. "Kyrie [3 voices] ... nota has figuras." (f. 80r)
34. *Inc.* "Quicumque voluerit discantare primo debet scire ..." *Exp.* "... ex una quinta perfecta et octava. et predicta patent in hoc exemplo [examples]." (ff. 80r–81r)
35. *Inc.* "[Q]uicumque vult cantare breviter et secure ..." *Exp.* "... certa discantus arte reperta. Deo gratias. Amen." (ff. 81v–82v)
36. *Tractatus figurarum. Inc.* "Incipit tractatus figurarum per quas diversimode discantatur per aliquos non sequentes modum tenoris sed alterius temporis. Quoniam sicut domino placuit ..." *Exp.* "... et si quatuor ascenderet usque ad octo et numerus sic deficeret. Sic itaque ad complementum huius operis secutus sum. ideo refero gratias Christo Amen." Additional section on *traynour. Inc.* "Vnc uidendum est qualiter ipsas ordinabimus ad discantandum diuersimode ..." *Exp.* "... in principio de tempore perfecto maiori ponuntur pro duobus temporibus novem semibreves vacue ut hic. trainer vel traineir [examples]." (ff. 84r–85v)
37. *Inc.* "Sequitur de sincopa. Unde sincopa est divisio ..." *Exp.* "... non tamen servatur in ipsis motettis. Et predicta quamvis rudia sufficiant in arte pratica cantus mensurabilis anellantibus introduci." (ff. 86r–87r)
38. *Tractatus figurarum* [fragment]. *Inc.* "Incipit tractatus figurarum per quas diversimode discantatur non sequentes ordinem tenoris sed alterius temporis. ut hic patet Quoniam sicut domino placuit ..." *Exp.* "... Consideret ergo unusquisque per uiam racionis quod omnis res plena atque perfecta si a plenitudine eius evacuetur non." (f. 87r)
39. *Inc.* "Sequitur de sincopa. Unde sincopa est divisio ..." *Exp.* "... non tamen servatur motettis. Exempla patent in motettis. Et hec predicta quamvis rudia sufficiant in arte pratica mensurabilis cantus anelantibus introducit." (ff. 88r–88v)
40. *Inc.* "Secundum magistrum Johannem de muris de modo perfecto. Nota quod quinque sunt partes prolationis ..." *Exp.* "... quando semibrevis valet duas minimas ut hic [example]." (ff. 88v–89r)
41. *Inc.* "Parti el monacordo in tre compassi ..." *Exp.* "... a quello istesso e vero compasso." (f. 92r)
42. *Inc.* "Sciendum est quod quatuor sunt tempora discantus ..." *Exp.* "... secunda similiter et tercia est brevis. Et hec sufficiant [examples]." (ff. 93r–94v)
43. *Inc.* "Incipiunt regule contrapuncti secundum magistrum Phylippottum de Caserta. Sciendum est quod contrapunctus est fundamentum discantj ..." *Exp.* "... non est falsa ymmo utilis. Expliciunt regule contrapuncti secundum magistrum phylippotum." (ff. 95v–96v)

44. *Inc.* "Et est sciendum quod in b fa ♮ mi ..." *Exp.* "... causa vero pulcritudinis ut patet in cantilenis. Et hec de contrapuncto sufficiant." (f. 97r)
45. *Inc.* "[P]ro introducione cognicionis habende de valloribus notularum ..." *Exp.* "... et per hoc sit finit abreviacionis de arte cantus." (ff. 99r–104v)
46. *Inc.* "Secuntur regule contrapunctus per supradictum magistrum facte sive ordinate ut sequitur. Pro noticia contrapunctus habenda primo sciendum est ..." *Exp.* "... utvi rev faIII laIus Et est finis deo gracias." (ff. 104v–107r)
47. *Inc.* "Quando tres minime pro semibreve ..." *Exp.* "... tunc est modus inperfectus ut hic [example] modus inperfectus." (f. 107v)
48. *Inc.* "Primo en gamaut ha tres consonantes ..." *Exp.* "... et apres .x. pos fer octava." (ff. 107v–108v)
49. *Inc.* "Ihesus Xristus Nota quod novem sunt species contrapunctus ..." *Exp.* "... ac si esset contrapunctus de natura [table]." (f. 110r–v)
50. *Inc.* "Pro introduccione cognicionis habende de valoribus notularum. Prima est sciendum ..." *Exp.* "... non tamen servatur in motectis." (ff. 111r–114r)
51. *Tractatus figurarum*. *Inc.* "Incipit tractatus figurarum per quas diversymody discantatur non sequentes ordinem tenoris sed alterius temporis. Quoniam sicut domino placuit ..." *Exp.* "... Et quatuor assenderit usque ad octo numerus sic defficeret Sic ipsum que ad complimentum vnius operis consequutus fuy Ideo refero gratias domino ihesu christo. Amen." (ff. 114r–116r)
52. *Inc.* "Nota quod quando quidem cantus ..." *Exp.* "... aumentationis est ut hic demonstretur [example]." (f. 116r)
53. *Inc.* "Incipit compendium artis mutectorum marchecty edictum abatis petro capuano de amalfia. Quoniam tocius nove artis motectorum ..." *Exp.* "... Et hec de arte mutechorum M. uniuscuiusque cantoris dubia resolventis sub compendio declarata sufficiant." (ff. 116r–117r)
54. *Inc.* "Ad evidentiam tam mensuralis quam inmensurabilis musice primo videndum est ..." *Exp.* "... tam assendendo quam dessendendo sane vel gradatim ut hic [example]." (ff. 117v–119v)
55. *Inc.* "De numeris musicalibus et de consonancijs in speciali tractatus. Ad videndum autem de numeris musicalibus ..." *Exp.* "... Alamire. grece nete iperboleon." (ff. 124r–128r)
56. Musical examples. "Maior perfectus ..." (ff. 128v–130r)
57. *Inc.* "Ihesus Christus filius tuus dominus noster. Ad habendum notitiam modorum seu tonorum ..." *Exp.* "... ex quo infertur quod autentiqus." (f. 137r–v)

In a study of lesser-known manuscript sources of music theory,[90] F. Alberto Gallo has described this codex and dated the contents to between the middle of the fourteenth and the beginning of the fifteenth century. With the exception of a Spanish music treatise, he believes that all the segments were copied in Italy. This is a composite codex whose contents were collected by Ferdinando Colombo during the first part of the sixteenth century and bound together in what the librarian thought to be chronological order in the second half of the seventeenth.[91] It contains two complete copies of the *Tractatus figurarum* (Se1 and Se3), as well as a fragment of the first portion (Se2). The manuscript also contains a commentary on the *Tractatus figurarum* published by Gallo in his *Mensurabilis musicae tractatuli*.[92]

The three copies contained in this manuscript are very good. The notation in Se1 is carefully preserved as well, and an interesting, extended set of examples of *traynour* is included at the end. Both for the number and quality of the sources of the *Tractatus figurarum*, and the commentary included, the Seville source is one of the most important.

Si

Siena, Biblioteca Comunale, L.V.30[93]

Paper; 150 folios, 30x22 cm
Italy; mid to late 15th century

1. Johannes de Muris, *Musica speculativa*. *Inc.* "[Q]uoniam musica est de numero ..." *Exp.* "... Explicit musica magistri iohannis de muris." (GS, 3:256–83) (ff. 1r–12v)
2. Diagram of intervals. (f. 13r; f. 13v blank)
3. Lambertus or Ps. Aristotle, *Musica*. *Inc.* "Sancti spiritus adsit nobis est. [Q]uoniam circa artem musicam ..." *Exp.* "... sicut in sequentibus patet exemplis ... sexquioctavus IX ad VIII." (ff. 14r–32r)
4. Table of pitches. (f. 32v)
5. Johannes de Muris, *Libellus cantus mensurabilis* [another hand has written the title]. *Inc.* "Incipit pratica cantus mensurabilis secundum Magistrum Johannem se Muris. Quilibet in arte ..." *Exp.* "... anelantibus introduci amen. Explicit pratica cantus mensurabilis

---

[90]Ibid., pp. 49–76.
[91]Ibid., p. 59.
[92]*Mensurabilis musicae tractatuli* (ed. Gallo).
[93]RISM BIII/2, pp. 120–23.

secundum magistrum iohannem de muris." (CS, 3:46–58) (ff. 33r–40v)

6. *Tractatus figurarum*. *Inc.* "Incipit tractatus diversarum figurarum, per quas diversimode discantatur non sequendo ordinem tenoris, sed alterius temporis secundum egidium de muris uel de murino. quoniam ut deo placuit ..." *Exp.* "... Et sic quatuor ascenerent usque otto et numerus deficeret et cetera. Sicque ad complementum huius operis consecutus sum. Ideo refero gratias deo." Additional section on *traynour*. *Inc.* "Qualiter ordinantur ad discantandum. Superius dictum est de aumentacione ..." *Exp.* "... Et primo de tempore perfecto maioris. ponuntur autem nouem semibreues uacue pro duobus temporibus ut hic [examples]." (ff. 41r–44r)

7. *Inc.* "Ordo ad componendum motettum cum cum tribus vel quatuor ..." *Exp.* "... in la debet esse quinta et retro habere clausum." (CS, 3:124–28) (ff. 44r–47r)

8. Ballata *Io vegio per staone* (Frater Antonius de Civitate). (ff. 47v–48r)

9. Marchetto, *Lucidarium* [compilation on proportions and consonances]. *Inc.* "Qui musica est scentia ..." *Exp.* "... numeri qui vocantur duces sunt numeri maiores, comites vero minores." (*Lucidarium* [ed. Herlinger]) (ff. 48v–56r)

10. Marchetto, *Pomerium*. *Inc.* "Incipit Pratica marchetti in musicha ..." *Exp.* "... quod tales cantus diversis coloribus figutentur, et hec sufficiant de musica mensurata." (*Pomerium* [ed. Vecchi]) (ff. 56v–91v)

11. Marchetto, *Lucidarium*. *Inc.* "Marchettus de padua. Lucidarium. Magnifici milites ..." *Exp.* "... Et hec de musica plana sufficiant ibi dicta. Amen. Explicit musica plana." (*Lucidarium* [ed. Herlinger]) (ff. 91v–119r)

12. *Inc.* "Nota quod VIIIem sunt littere ..." *Exp.* "... non cessant ymnum cantare scilicet Sanctus etcetera." (CS, 1:253a; 4:204a) (ff. 119r–120v)

13. Ascribed to Guido. *Inc.* "Est tonus in numeris ..." *Exp.* "... loca cuius idipsum." (GS, 2:32–33) (ff. 120v–121r)

14. Guido, *Micrologus* [Metrologus sive Expositio]. *Inc.* "Guidus de Sancto Mauro. In nomine sancte ..." *Exp.* "... modorumque varias qualitates (?)" (ff. 121r–127r)

15. Table of solmization. (f. 127r–v)

16. "Dicendum est quod ista figura ... " (ff. 127v–129r)

17. *Inc.* "De prima differentia nulla datur ..." *Exp.* "... re ut re mi re quaternus." (CS, 1:262a) (f. 129r)

18. Philippe de Vitry, *Compendium artis novae*. *Inc.* "Sub brevissimo compendio philippo de vitriaco in musica incipit ..." *Exp.* "... quia tunc ponuntur ad differentiam prolationis ut hic patet." (CS, 3:29a–34a) *Inc.* "Hoc versos disce qui in cantus discere cupis. Ante namque longa ..." *Exp.* "... secunda dupletur. (CS, 3:262b) Explicit philipus

de vitriaco." (ed. by G. Reaney in *Musica Disciplina* 14 [1960]: 30–31) (f. 129r–v)

19. Bernardus Cisterciensis. *Inc.* "Psalmodia non nimium protendamus ..." *Exp.* "... semper bona pausa faciamus." (f. 129v)

20. *De proportionibus musicalibus,* a treatise from the music theory of Johannes de Muris and compiled by Petrus de Sancto Dionysio. *Inc.* "Tractatus de proportionibus. Tractatus fratris petri de Sancto dionisio ..." *Exp.* "... epogdoa grece latine dicitur sesquiottava et hic terminatur proportiones declarate." (de Muris, *Notitia* [ed. Michels]) (ff. 129v–135v)

21. Another treatise on proportions, chiefly taken from Marchetto's *Lucidarium. Inc.* "Tractatus de proportionibus ..." *Exp.* "... ut sunt decem et otto ad novem sub tali signo 2/1 ut hic [example] Explicit." (ff. 135r–142v)

22. *Inc.* "Sub brevissimo compendio Bernardus de Clygny in musica incipit. Omnis nota ..." *Exp.* "... sunt breves." (CS, 3:262ab) *Inc.* "De modo perfecto ..." *Exp.* "... et tunc non alteratur sed perficitur. finis. Explicit." (ff. 142v–143r)

23. *Inc.* "Alique demontrationes in proportionibus. Minima in musica dicitur figura ..." *Exp.* "... dicunt fore sexquialteram maiorem." (ff. 143v–144r)

24. Commentary on Boethius' *Musica. Inc.* "Primum atque secundum capitulum prohemii artis musice boetii hoc continet ..." *Exp.* "... atque examinavit pondus malleorum et quia erant fortis finis. Explicit." (ff. 144r–146r)

25. Johannes Hothby, *Tractatus de contrapuncto. Inc.* "Tractatus de contrapuncto ..." *Exp.* "... quoniam tunc non vocatur contrapunctus gratia ipsius contrapuncti sed gratia tenoris. Explicit ars contrapuncti." [The codex ends with memory verses] "C naturam dat – fb molle tibi signat – gb quadrum – sit tibi caniturum." (CS, 1:256a) (ff. 146v–150r; f. 150v blank; I–IV blank)

Herlinger believes this manuscript to be written in a single, humanistic hand from the mid- to the late-fifteenth century.[94] Aside from the Italianate spellings, the text of the *Tractatus figurarum* is good. This is also one of the few sources in which the copyist clearly took care in preserving the notation, giving variants when possible.[95] Under these circumstances, it is not surprising that an expanded set of examples of *traynour* is appended to the *Tractatus figurarum*.

---

[94]*Lucidarium* (ed. Herlinger), p. 34.
[95]Chapter 6 (see 82.12 and 88.4, for example).

Wa

Washington, Library of Congress, ML171.J6[96]

Paper; 173 folios, 21x15 cm
Northern Italy; 1465–1489

1. Circular astronomical chart, after which follows: *Inc.* "Questo e el corso de li pianeti quanti anni ..." *Exp.* "... Luna sempio pianeta e sta soto tute le altre pianeta a presso ala terra el quale sta in ciascaduno segno per doy di e mezo. et (?) formisse el corso so in trenta di." (f. [i]$^{r-v}$)
2. Astronomical figure, after which is read: "Ipsa ego sum johannis francisci [one word scraped] ex scripta in usum/ Qui propria exscripsit me quoque iure tenet." (f. [ii]^r)
3. "Liber mei fassoni fassati ex conditionis cuniolii legum scholaris studentis in regia civitate papie domini 1489 die." (f. [ii]^v)
4. *Inc.* "Ista est quedam ratio Paschalis ..." *Exp.* "... Qui finise la suprascripta tavela a trovare la pascha. scripta per don johanne francesco da pavia 1477, nonas octobris." (ff. a–c)
5. *Inc.* "Si vis invenire locam dominicalem debes notare hanc rotas presentes ..." *Exp.* "... Et sic decetero annuati procedendo cognosces proculdubio qui sit locam dominicalis. et quando bisextus occurat usque in eternum et in seculum seculi. Explicit rubrica." (ff. c^v–h^r)
6. Index of the book. *Inc.* "In isto libelo continentur omnia infrascripta ..." *Exp.* "... septimo et ultimo opus M. Johannis de muris de Arte contra[puncto]." (f. h^v)
7. Index of the chapters of the *Lucidarium* of Marchetto. *Inc.* "Incipit capitula lucidarii Marcheti de padua..." *Exp.* "... de principys primi toni capitulum 6 in folio 35." (f. h^v–k^r; f. k^v blank)
8. Marchetto, *Lucidarium*. *Inc.* "Incipit epistola Marcheti de Padua. Magnifico militi et potenti domino suo ..." *Exp.* "... per suum nuntium praticari. Et hec de musica plana dicta ibi sufficiant. Explicit. Explicit lucidarium Marcheti de padua quod scripsit dominus Johannes franciscus de papia monachus Venerabilis cenobii sancti Georgii de Venetiis. 1465." (*Lucidarium* [ed. Herlinger]) (ff. 1r–47r)
9. *Inc.* "Hic continentur manus greca, latina atque contrapunti ..." *Exp.* "... Ad te nos de pro tria. vt re mi fa sol la."(f. 47v)
10. Johannes de Muris, *Libellus cantus mensurabilis*. *Inc.* "Ex tractatu magistri Johannis de Muris de pratica arte mensurabilis cantus. Quilibet

---

[96]Description based on Hothby, *De arte contrapuncti* (ed. Reaney), pp. 17–21.

in arte pratica mensurabilis cantus erudiri mediocriter affectans ..."
Exp. "... in arte pratica mensurabilis cantus volentibus introduci. Gratias deo refferamus nostro. Explicit ars cantus mensurabilis secundum magistrum Johannem de Muris, quam scripsit dominus Johannes franciscus preotonus papiensi[s] monachus ... qui vivit et regnat in secula seculorum." (ff. 47v–56r)

11. Johannes de Garlandia. *Inc.* "Ex tractatu magistri de galadia de musica plana. Pro introductione artis musice. Primo videndum est quod est introductio ..." *Exp.* "... et si cantus medietatem utriusque incipiat, tunc proprie dicitur esse mixtus, et non aliter. Explicit ars cantus plani magistri Johannis de galadia, quam scripsit dominus Johannes franciscus de papia monachus monastrii sancti georgii de venetiis, 1465 die sancti Syri." (ff. 56r–70r)

12. *Inc.* "Alique regule utiles in cantu firmo sive plano. Nota quod quando cantus ascendit ab E grave vel G grave ..." *Exp.* "... vocibus ascendunt, quamvis totidemque subibunt. Explicit." (f. 70r–v)

13. *Tractatus figurarum. Inc.* "Incipit tractatus diversarum figurarum per quas diversimodi discantantur non sequendo ordinem tenoris sed (?) alterius temporis secundum Egidium monachum. Prologus incipit. Quoniam ut deo placuit ..." *Exp.* "... et si quatuor ascenderent usque ad octo et nunc sic deficerent. Sic itaque ad complementum huius operis consecutus sum. Ideo refero gratias deo. Amen." Additional section on *traynour. Inc.* "Superius dictum est de augmentatione ..." *Exp.* "... et primo de tempori perfecto maioris. et ponuntur pro duobus temporibus nouem semibreues vacue. vt hic de tempori perfecto maiori [examples]. De modo componendi tenores motetorum. Capitulum quartum. Primo accipe tenorem alciciuius antiphone ... Explicit tractatus magistri Egidii mensurabilis cantus, quem scripsit dominus Johannes franciscus ... venetiis 1465. (*De modo componendi*, CS, 3:124–28) Superius dictum est de augmentacione atque diminutione figurarum. Nunc dicendum est quale ipsas ordinabis ad discantandum diversimode ... Et primo de tempore perfecto maioris et ponuntur pro duobus temporibus noues semibreues vacue ut hic infra patet [examples]."[97] (ff. 70v–79v; f. 80r blank)

14. Hand of Guido. (f. 80v)

15. Johannes de Anglia, *Tractatus de arte contrapuncte. Inc.* "Incipit primus tractatus de arte contrapuncti. Secundum venerabilem priorem dominum Johannem de Anglia. quem ipse direxit ad venerabilem monachum domnum Johannem franciscum de preotonibus de papia. et ut melius et adiscatur atque intelligatur in lingua materna descripsit ac notavit ponendo tenorem in nigro colore et contratenorem in rubeo. Et

---

[97]As in Lo and Ro5, the *Tractatus figurarum* is conjoined to the *Tractatus cantus mensurabilis* after which, however, the additional section on *traynour* is repeated.

primo de primo gradu ..." *Exp.* "... post unam consonantiam perfectam debemus facere imperfectam. Explicit sumula de arte contrapuncti quam scripsit don Johannes franciscus preottonus de papia ad laudem dei. Amen." (Hothby, *De arte contrapunti* [ed. Reaney], pp. 15–49) (ff. 81r–95v)

16. *Inc.* "Incipit brevis sumula de arte mensurabilis cantus. Primus et ante omnia scire debes quod quinque sunt figurae notularum in musicha. Prima vocatur minima ..." *Exp.* "... Explicit ars musicae sub brevi quam scripsit don johannes franciscus ... per infinita saecula saeculorum. Amen." (ff. 96r–98r)

17. Verse. *Inc.* "Guido monachus composuit. His sex formantur ..." *Exp.* "... C. naturam. F. quoque .b. molle. Amen." (f. 98r)

18. Table of divisions according to prolatio and tempus. (ff. 98v–100r)

19. Hand of Guido. (f. 100v)

20. *Inc.* "Ratio Guidonis monachi. Nota quod 22e litterae sunt in manu Guidonis ..." *Exp.* "... secundum rectum vocabulum gramaticalem ponitur dia. pro duo. Explicit." (f. 101r–v)

21. *Inc.* "De formationibus tonorum. Primus tonus continet suam undecimam aliquando ..." *Exp.* "... omnium sanctorum et sanctarum dei. Deo gratias. Amen." (ff. 101v–102r)

22. *Inc.* "Versus. III pares ut plurimum ascendere debent ..." *Exp.* "... per tres per quatuor vel quinque notas." (f. 102r–v)

23. Petrus de Sancto Dionysio, *Tractatus de cantu mensurabili. Inc.* "Incipit tractatus fratris Petri de sancto dionisio qui est in duas partes ..." *Exp.* "... Explicit pars cantus fratris petri de sancto dionisio quam scripsit don Jo. franc. preottonus de papia." (de Muris, *Notitia* [ed. Michels]) (ff. 102v–109r)

24. *Ubi karitas et amor* [for three voices]. (ff. 109v–110r)

25. *Jesu dolce o infinit amor* [with music]. (f. 110v; f. 111r–v blank)

26. Johannes de Muris, *Ars contrapuncti. Inc.* "Tractatus Johannis de muris de arte contrapuncti. Quilibet affectans scientiam contrapuncti ..." *Exp.* "... sed si scire vis in quo tempore sit facta vide et quere diminutiones ipsius." (CS, 3:59–68) (ff. 112r–117v)

27. *Inc.* "Sequitur de tertio membro huius artis. Nota quod unisonus de ut est simile ..." *Exp.* "... Explicit tractatus magistri Johannis de Muris quem scripsit don Johannes franciscus ... Deo gratias Amen. Sorte supernorum scriptor libri potiatur Morte infernorum raptor libri moriatur. Iste liber est mei fassoni fassati ex dominis cuniolii patria ... 1507 de mense februarii questoriae dignitati ascitus in ea per transii usque ad." (ff. 117v–119r)

28. Diverse modulatio for two voices. (ff. 119v–128r)

29. *Inc.* "Qui se incomenza La raxone e le questione de la littera canzelarescha ..." *Exp.* "... fosse menado a mezza pena. oXo och[?] la

fileta non porent andare in fin de quela asta." (ff. 128v–133r; ff. 133v–137v blank)

30. Guido, *Micrologus. Inc.* "Incipit Michrologus id est brevis sermo in musica editus a domno Guidone musico. Gymnasio musas ..." *Exp.* "... per cuncta viget in saecula Amen. Explicit are musicae guidonis quam scripsit dom johannes franciscus ... secundo martii." (Guido of Arezzo, *Micrologus,* ed. Joseph Smits van Waesberghe, Corpus scriptorum de musica, no. 4 [n.p.: American Institute of Musicology, 1955]) (ff. 138r–155r)

31. *Inc.* "Temporibus nostris super omnes homines ..." *Exp.* "... ex industria componantur." (GS, 2:34–37a) (ff. 155v–157v)

32. From a letter of Guido to Michael. *Inc.* "Qui vero monochordum desiderat facere ..." *Exp.* "... studeat intelligere (GS, 2:46a) [A]d inveniendum igitur ignotum cantum ... in qua neuma finita est." (GS, 2:44b–45b) (ff. 157v–159r; f. 159v blank)

33. *Inc.* "Iesus. Calmetta. Ergine dietro a la producta prole ..." *Exp.* "... cum supprema humilta supprema sede [?]" (f. 160r; ff. 160v–164v blank)

34. Guido, *Regulae rhythmicae. Inc.* "Incipiunt rithimi don Vuidonis Musici de gretia et primo de plana musica in monochordo. Musicorum et cantorum ..." *Exp.* "... quin sit idem semper melum in una et altera." (GS, 2:25–33) (ff. 165r–170v)

35. *Inc.* "Omnes autenti quinto loco a se principia ..." *Exp.* "... et fines distinctionum partium atque syllabarum." (ff. 170v–171r)

36. *Inc.* "Feci regulas apertas ..." *Exp.* "... gloria sit domino. Amen." (GS, 2:33) (ff. 171v–172r)

37. *Inc.* "Ars humanas instruit loquelas ..." *Exp.* "... dum carent proportionibus." (CS, 2:110–11a) (f. 172r–v; 173r blank)

The portion of the manuscript containing the *Tractatus figurarum* was written by Johannes Franciscus Preottonus at St. George's, Venice in 1465.[98] In fact, most of the manuscript appears to have been written between 1465 and 1477. There is a very close connection between Wa and Ro5. The slavishness with which the Wa source follows Ro5 suggests direct copying. Nevertheless, some correction of errors consistent with other sources reveals either that Preottonus had more than one source with which to work or that an intervening copy of the *Tractatus figurarum* exists from which Wa copied.

---

[98]*Lucidarium* (ed. Herlinger), p. 39.

The Stemma

At present, fourteen copies of the *Tractatus figurarum* are known to have survived to the present day. One source, cited by Coussemaker in his *Scriptores*,[99] is the Codex Vindobonensis.[100] All copies but one contain complete versions of the text. The only fragmentary source occurs in the manuscript now located in Sevilla, Catedral Metropolitana Biblioteca Capitular y Colombina, which contains two other complete copies of the treatise as well. This fascinating collection of manuscripts was part of the Biblioteca Columbia, a library whose books were collected by Ferdinando Colombo during the first part of the sixteenth century in his travels across Europe. This particular volume was bound in the second half of the seventeenth century, the binder arranging various musical treatises in what he considered to be chronological order.[101] A few of the fourteen *Tractatus* sources contain the dates and names of those who copied them, but most appear to be anonymous fifteenth-century Italian copies. One source, however, was copied as late as the eighteenth century by Johann Christoph Pepusch from the manuscript Cotton Tiberius B.IX of the British Library.[102] The original from which Pepusch copied was almost completely destroyed by fire. Its remains, however, have been dated to the late fourteenth century, making the Pepusch manuscript a copy of one of the earliest known sources.[103]

A comparison of the sources reveals the existence of at least fifteen additional lost sources, with a great probability of others surviving not associated with this stemma. Moreover, a direct relationship can be demonstrated between only two of the sources. There are, however, three clear traditions (grouped as A, B, and Γ in the following discussion). The difficulty arises in attempting to relate these traditions to one another and to the few sources that remain outside them. In the following discussion, demonstrations will be given both for the three traditions and the relationships of the manuscripts within each. An attempt will then be made to organize them into a complete stemma.

---

[99]CS, 3:xxiii-xxiv.

[100]Kurt von Fischer, "Eine wiederaufgefundene Theoretikerhandschrift des späten 14. Jahrhunderts," *Schweizer Beiträge zur Musikwissenschaft* 1 (1972): 23.

[101]Gallo, "Alcune fonti," p. 59.

[102]Arlt, p. 38.

[103]Ibid.

The A group consists of four sources: Lo, Ro5, Si, and Wa. The strongest factor in grouping these sources together is their attribution of the *Tractatus* to Egidius de Murino or Egidius Monachus.[104] In fact, the *Tractatus figurarum* is followed by Egidius's treatise *De modo componendi* in each source and is often conjoined by a continuous numbering of their chapters. Other than this, these four are closely associated by a number of textual variants and insertions peculiar to them. For instance, in chapter 3 (74.1), there is a discussion of the hollowing out or imperfection of a semibrevis in which group A substitutes the more graphic phrase "si eius venter evacuetur" for the more mundane "si inventa fuerit vacua."

This group contains the only directly related pair of sources in the stemma. Both Ro5 and Wa contain a number of variants peculiar to them alone. Perhaps the most striking occurs during the discussion in chapter 6 (82.12–84.2) of a note shape of which two are used to replace nine minimae. They are described as being a combination of a dotted semibrevis and a semiminima as their shape reveals. Yet Ro5 and Wa break them into their component parts (that is, two semibreves and two semiminimae), thus introducing four notes instead of two. From the number of variants that occur in Wa which do not appear in Ro5, it is clear that Wa was copied either directly from Ro5 or from another source, itself a copy of Ro5. There are also a number of variants peculiar to Lo, Si, and Wa, thus establishing some sort of contamination in the copying of Wa, an all too common occurrence in the stemma of this treatise. Based on the evidence summarized above, the relationship between the sources in group A can be charted with a fair degree of confidence as follows:

---

[104] "... secundum Magistrum Egidium de Muris vel de Morino" (Lo), "... secundum egidium de muris vel de murino" (Si), "... secundum Egidium monachum" (Wa).

Nearly all copies of the *Tractatus figurarum* have a place following Johannes de Muris's *Libellus* in the manuscripts in which they occur, a few even confusing the names Murino and Muris.[105] The sources do vary, however, in what follows the *Tractatus,* and this can occasionally be useful in determining a tradition as in A above. A similar case exists for the manuscripts in group B (Fa, Na, Pi, and Ro1), for in each manuscript the *Tractatus figurarum* is followed by the *Ars contrapuncti* attributed to de Muris.[106] In three of the four manuscripts, the *Tractatus figurarum* remains anonymous, with only Fa attributing it to Philippus de Caserta. As this is the only source to contain this attribution and there is slight evidence that Fa was copied from Pi (which does not contain this attribution), little faith can be placed in the veracity of this statement. The manuscripts of group B, then, are unified in their lack of attribution to Egidius, their sequence of copying, and a number of omissions and substitutions unique to them. Within this grouping, one finds a subset of variants peculiar to Fa, Pi, and Ro1 (and a smaller number peculiar to only Fa and Pi), yielding the stemma below. A close relative of

---

[105]"Incipit tractatus diversarum figurarum, per quas diversimode discantatur non sequendo ordinem tenoris, sed alterius temporis secundum egidium de muris uel de murino" (Si); "... secundum Magistrum Egidium de Muris vel de Morino" (Lo).

[106]Ulrich Michels, *Die Musiktraktate des Johannes de Muris,* Beihefte zum *Archiv für Musikwissenschaft,* vol. 8 (Wiesbaden: Franz Steiner, 1970), pp. 40–42.

the group is Se1. Because of the composite nature of the Seville manuscript, it is often impossible to tell what follows a particular treatise, and so an important criterion is lost. At times, though, Se1 shares the variants unique to this group and so appears to have been derived from the same source as group B.

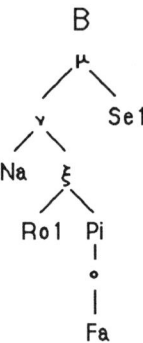

The members of Γ (Ca, Mi, and Se3) are unified only in that they share many of the same variants, such as the conflation of text in chapter 8 (92.10–94.2). Se1, at times, shares variants with Γ that do not show up in B, thus revealing some sort of contamination with this group. Se2 occasionally shares variants with this group as well, implying some sort of connection. All are accounted for in the following diagram:

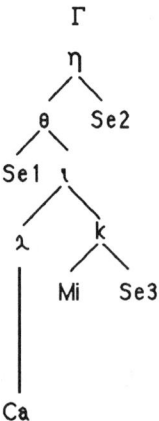

The only source not mentioned as yet is Ch, which defies placement in any of these groupings. In many ways, this is unfortunate, for Ch is one of the earliest sources and its version of the text and examples is often excellent. It will, however, occasionally share variants with group A and so is shifted towards it in the completed stemma.

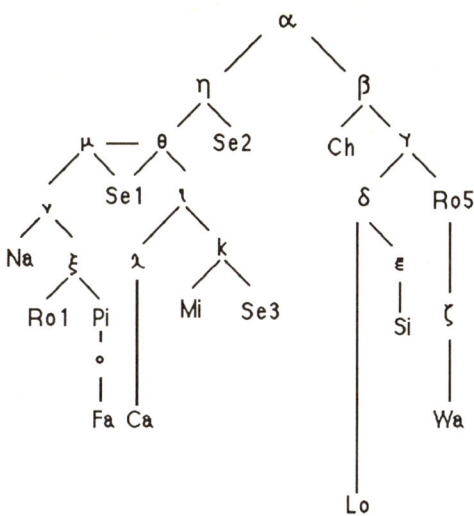

The Edition

In the compilation of this edition, a balance was sought between the exacting nature of a critical edition and the cumbersomeness of over-editing. Variants of a purely orthographical nature have not been noted, nor have a few cases of meaningless word substitutions (*et* for *adque*, or the reverse) and obvious grammatical errors, if they could not be construed to alter the meaning of the text. No mention has been made of variations in word order and the medieval orthography is retained. A minimum of punctuation has been included in the Latin text. The sources themselves vary tremendously as to their punctuation, which in turn creates slight changes in the meaning of the text. Since the editor's choice of punctuation is apparent from the parallel English translation, it was felt the text could profitably remain free from this intrusion.

The chapter divisions in the various sources of the *Tractatus figurarum* vary a great deal. For this reason, a new and consistent numbering has been adopted with the original chapter numbering of all sources appearing in the notes.

The present edition is based upon a collation of all fourteen copies of the treatise. The text appears at the top of each verso page and the variant readings at the bottom. The translation appears on the facing recto pages, with comments designed to elucidate the text below. Great care has been taken to insure the consistent handling of technical terms and to provide a readable, yet faithful translation.

CONSPECTUS CODICUM ET NOTARUM

Manuscripts

Ch	Chicago, Newberry Library, Ms. 54.1 (1391), **US-Cn**
Se1-3	Sevilla, Catedral Metropolitana, Biblioteca Capitular y Colombina, 5.2.25 (mid 14th to early 15th century), **E-Sc(a)**
Ro5	Roma, Biblioteca Apostolica Vaticana, lat. 5321 (late 14th to early 15th century), **I-Rvat**
Ro1	Roma, Biblioteca Apostolica Vaticana, Palatinus lat. 1377 (late 14th century), **I-Rvat**
Pi	Pisa, Biblioteca Universitaria, Ms. 606 II (after 1411), **I-PIu**
Fa	Faenza, Biblioteca Comunale, Ms. 117 (1473-74), **I-FZe**
Si	Siena, Biblioteca Comunale, L.V.30 (mid to late 15th century), **I-Sc**
Wa	Washington, Library of Congress, ML171.J6 (1465–89), **US-Wc**
Na	Napoli, Biblioteca Nazionale, Ms. VIII D 12 (15th century), **I-Nn**
Mi	Milano, Biblioteca Ambrosiana, Ms. I 20 inf. (after 1440), **I-Ma**
Ca	Catania, Biblioteche Riunite Civica e Antonio Ursino Recupero, Ursino Recupero D.39 (1473), **I-CATc**
Lo	London, British Library, Additional 4909 (early 18th century), **GB-Lbm**

Earlier Edition

CS *Scriptorum de musica medii aevi nova series a Gerbertina altera*, 4 vols., ed. Edmond de Coussemaker (Paris: Durand, 1864–76; reprint ed., Hildesheim: Olms, 1963), 3:118–24.

Notes

add.	adds		*sep.*	separate
ante	before		*sine*	without
cap.	chapter		*tit.*	title
cett.	the rest		*vac.*	hollow
ex.	example			
fig.	noteshape		⟨⟩ enclose text supplied by the editor or from a parallel source.	
in marg.	in the margin			
lon.	longa			
min.	minima			
om.	omitted			
permut.	are interchanged			
pl.	filled			
pr.	first			
punc.	dot			
rub.	red			
scripsi	I have written			
sec.	second			
semibr.	semibrevis			

⟨TRACTATUS FIGURARUM⟩

⟨PROLOGUS⟩

Incipit tractatus figurarum per quas diversimode discantatur non sequentes ordinem tenoris sed alterius temporis. Quoniam sicut domino placuit scientiam musice in corde desiderantium gratiose perlustravit. Et licet magistri nostri antiqui primum intellectum musicalem habuerunt, et hoc satis grosso modo sicut adhuc patet in motetis ipsorum magistrorum videlicet *Tribum que non abhor‖ruit*, et in aliis et cetera. Tamen ipsi post modum sub-

---

Tit.: Tractatus figurarum *scripsi* Tractatus Magistri Phillipoti Andree artis nove Ch Alius tractatulus de musica incerto authore Lo *om. cet.* ‖ 2 Prologus *scripsi* ‖ 3 figurarum]philippi de caserta de diversis figuris Fa diversarum figurarum LoSiWa | diversimode]dulces modi Lo diversimodi Se3Wa | discantatur]discantantur LoNaWa discantatur per aliquos Ro1Se1 discantantur per aliquas Na discantatur per aliquas Pi discantatur per aliquas regulas Fa | non]et ideo Lo ‖ 3–4 Incipit ... temporis *om.* CaChRo5 ‖ 4 sequentes] sequendo LoSiWa | ordinem]modum FaNaPiRo1Se1 | tenoris]tenorum Ro1 | sed]scilicet Lo | temporis]tenoris Fa temporibus Na temporis ut hic patet Se2 temporis secundum egidium de muris vel de murino Si temporis secundum Magistrum Egidium de Muris vel de Morino Lo temporis secundum Egidium monachum. Prologus incipit Wa | Quoniam]qui Lo | sicut]ut LoSiWa | domino]deo ChLoMiSiWa ‖ 5 scientia CaSi | musicalem Lo | corda ChLo SiWa cordo Na | desiderantium]desideratum Lo desidentium vel desideratium Se1 | gratiose]gloriose CaLoSi | perlustravit]perlustravit et cetera Ro5 perlustrare Wa | licet *om.* FaNaPiRo1 ‖ 6 primum]suum Wa | intelligendum musicam Ca | habuerint Ro5Wa ‖ 7 grosso]gratiose Ro5Wa | sicut]sed Lo | patet *om.* ChSe 2 | ipsorum]eorum Si | magistrorum]magistrorum uel antiquorum Ch magistrorum antiquorum LoSe1Wa *om.* MiSi | videlicet] videlicet in CaChLoMiRo5Se1-3Si ‖ 8 abhorruit et in aliis]abhorruit et in rex carole, ac etiam in aliis motetis Fa | et in aliis *om.* MiSi ‖ aliis]multis Se2 | et cetera *om.* FaLoNaPiRo1Ro5Se2 | Tamen]cum Ro1 | post modum *om.* Mi ‖ 8–68.1 modum subtiliorem *om.* Se3 | subtiliter Na ‖

TREATISE ON NOTESHAPES

PROLOGUE

Here begins the treatise on noteshapes[1] through which, in various ways, lines are discanted that do not follow the order of the tenor but of another tempus.[2] Since it pleased the Lord, he graciously illumined the knowledge of music in the heart of those desiring it. Granted that our venerable masters held a most excellent musical understanding—and this sufficient for the grand manner as hitherto is shown in the motets of these very same masters, namely, *Tribum que non abhorruit*[3] and in others, et cetera—yet they them-

---

[1] By noteshapes (*figurae*), the author means to discuss the physical manifestation of a note, that is, its shape.

[2] As the treatise proceeds, it is clear the intent is to be able to notate an upper voice in a mensuration other than that of the tenor by a system of *figurae* designed to produce the aural effect of an equal brevis between the two lines while notationally retaining an equal minima.

[3] A motet by the most illustrious musician of his day, Philippe de Vitry, most likely cited for its use of undifferentiated semibreves (see p. 10 n. 31).

tiliorem modum considerantes, primum relinquerunt, et artem magis subtiliter ordinaverunt ut patet in *Apta caro*. Sic nunc successive venientes, habentes et intelligentes que primi magistri relinquerunt maiores subtili||tates per studium sunt confecti ut quod per antecessores imperfectum relictum fuit

5 per successores reformetur.

CS3: 119a

CAPITULUM PRIMUM

DE FIGURIS A MAGISTRIS TRADITIS

Nunc itaque figure a magistris nostris relicte sunt quasi omnibus manifeste, videlicet duplex longa ▬┐ longa ▬┐ brevis ▬■▬ semibrevis ◆

10 et minima ↧

---

1 modum]modo Se3 *om*. NaPiRo1 | considerantes]comparantes Fa | primum]prime Na primam Si primum modum magistri Se1 *om*. Ro5 | reliquerunt LoRo1Se1-3Wa | artem *om*. Ro5Wa | magis]magistri Lo magnam Se3 *om*. Si ‖ 1–2 subtilior Lo subtiliorem Si ‖ 1–4 considerantes … confecti]considerantes et tractantes primo reliquerunt maioris subtilitatis per studium converti Ca ‖ 2 ordinaverunt]invenerunt Si ordinaverunt quod Mi | ut patet]et Se3 | in]in moteto Fa in isto moteto Ro1 | caro et cetera ChRo1Se2-3Si caro et in aliis et cetera Wa | Sic]Sicut NaPiRo1Se1Se3 sed Wa | venientes] venientes acurorem intellectum Si venientes acutiorem intellectum LoWa ‖ 2–3 sic … relinquerunt *om*. Ca | venientes habentes et *om*. ChFa | habentes *om*. Ro5 ‖ 3 et … que]et magis intelligentes ea que Si | que]qui Ch quod Ro5 | primi *om*. Ro5 | reliquerunt PiRo1Ro5Se1-3 relinquerunt per LoSiWa | maiores]maiores inde Fa | subtilitas Se3 ‖ 3–4 per studium sunt confecti]invenerunt FaNaPiRo1Se1 ‖ 4 studium]studium moderni Si | sunt confecti]sunt auctores facti Wa *om*. Ro5 | confecti]consequti Ch consecuti LoSe2Si | ut]ut hoc ChRo5Wa ut haec Lo | ut … antecessores]ut hec que aprimi (?) antecessores Si | quod *om*. Se3 | imperfectum]secundum Ca *om*. Ch | imperfecta relicta sunt Si | fuit]est FaPiRo1Se1 sint Ro5 *om*. Na ‖ 5 reformatur Se3 reformentur Si ‖ 6 Capitulo primo MiPiRo1Se1Se2 *om*. Wa ‖ 6–7 Capitulum … traditis *om*. CaChFaLoNaRo5 ‖ 7 De … traditis *om*. Se2-3 | magistris]magistris nostris Ro1 | traditis et de pausationibus Si ‖ 8 Nunc itaque figure]De figuris Na | itaque]igitur CaFaPiRo1 itaque successive Wa | magistribus Si | nostris *om*. CaFaLoSi | relicte]tradite LoRo5SiWa | omnis Si ‖ 8–9 manifeste]manifestis Ca manifeste iste Se3 ‖ 8–10 manifeste … minima]manifeste unde pro duplici longa, pro longa, pro brevi, pro semibrevi, pro minima Wa ‖ 9 duplici Mi | longa (*sec.*) *om*. Ca ‖ 9–10 *figg. vac.* Ro5 (*minima pl.*)Se3(*longa om.*) *om*. Ca ‖ 10 minima et sufficit Ca minima cum suis pausis Fa minima et cetera Mi ‖

selves, after considering a manner to be a more subtle manner, abandoned the earlier manner and created an art more subtly, as is shown in *Apta caro*.[4] So, since those who come later hold and understand the things that the earlier masters leave behind, greater subtleties are accomplished through earnest striving so that what was left imperfect by our predecessors may be reformed by their followers.

CHAPTER ONE

ON THE NOTESHAPES HANDED DOWN BY THE MASTERS[5]

Now, these are the noteshapes left by our masters as apparent to all, namely, the duplex longa ⟶ longa ⟶ brevis ⟶ semibrevis ⟶ and minima ⟶

---

[4]A popular motet from circa 1360 notable for the complexity of its isorhythm and free use minimae (see p. 11 n. 34).

[5]This is the standard set of *figurae* established by Johannes de Muris (cf. *Johannis de Muris Notitia artis musicae et compendium musicae practicae, Petrus* [sic] *de Sancto Dionysio Tractatus de musica*, ed. Ulrich Michels, Corpus scriptorum de musica, no. 17 [n.p.: American Institute of Musicology, 1972], pp. 78–79, 119–34). The exclusion of the semiminima is surprising as it is to play so important a rôle in the author's notational system. Its omission is certainly a conservative trait, for although it is omitted from some mid-century theoretical treatises (e.g., *Ars [musicae] Johannis Boen*, ed. F. Alberto Gallo, Corpus scriptorum de musica, no. 19 [(Rome): American Institute of Musicology, 1972]), it does appear in others (*Tractatulus de cantu mensurali seu figurativo musice artis*, ed. F. Alberto Gallo, Corpus scriptorum de musica, no. 16 [(Rome): American Institute of Musicology, 1971], p. 17).

CAPITULUM SECUNDUM

DE PAUSATIONIBUS

Pausa duplicis longe ▦ longe ▤ brevis ══ semibrevis ══ et minime ══ Ex istis quedam perfecte et quedam imperfecte reperiuntur
5 ubique quasi scripte. Et licet magistri instruxerunt nos in his figuris ac etiam in quatuor mensuris principalibus, videlicet in tempore perfecto maioris prolationis et in tempore imperfecto ipsius, in tempore perfecto minoris prolationis et in tempore imperfecto ipsius. Tamen non docuerunt quomodo super tempus imperfectum minoris discantare deberemus perfectum minoris, et e
10 converso, et sic de singulis temporibus quod clare singulariter inferius pate-

---

1 Capitulum secundum]Capitulo secundo MiSe3 Capitulum primum Wa *om.* NaPiRo1Se1 ‖ 1–2 Capitulum ... pausationibus *om.* CaFaRo5Se2Si ‖ 2 De pausationibus]De pausis capitulum primum Lo ‖ 3 duplici ChMiSe3Si | ▦] ▤ Ch ▦ FaSe2 ▦ Se3 | ▤] ▤ ChFaLoNaPiRo1Se2-3 | ⊥] ⊥ Ro1 ‖ 3–4 Pausa duplicis ... et minime]Pausa duplex longa, longa, minima NaPiRo1Se1-3 Pausa pro duplici longa, pro longa, pro brevi, pro semibrevi, pro minima Wa *om.* CaFa ‖ 4 ⊥] ⊥ Ro1 | minima et cetera MiRo1Se2-3 | *ante* Ex istis]Et quedam imperfecte capitulo secundo MiSe1 Quidam imperfectis Se2 Et quidem imperfecte CaSe3 | istis]istis sunt ChRo5 | quedam (*pr.*)]quidam Se3 | quedam perfecte et *om.* Ca | et quedam imperfecte *om.* FaMiNaPiRo1Se1-3 | quedam (*sec.*)]quidam Ca | imperfectione Ca | reperitur Mi ‖ 5 ubique]ubique id est Wa | quasi *om.* Ro1 | descripte Ro1 inscripte Ca | licet]licet hii FaPi hii Ro1 *om.* Ch | magistris Na | introduxerunt Se3 instruxerint Fa | his]istis CaMi ‖ 6 videlicet *om.* Mi | in tempore *om.* Wa ‖ 6–7 in tempore perfecto maioris prolationis et *om.* Mi | prolationis *om.* Se2-3 ‖ 7 ipsius]maioris prolationis LoSe1SiWa eiusdem Fa ‖ 7–8 prolationis *om.* CaMiPiSe1-3Si ‖ 8 in tempore *om.* Wa | imperfecto]perfecto Na | ipsius]minoris Se1Si minoris prolationis Lo minorum eiusdem Fa | Tamen]Sed Ro5 | docuerunt nos Ch | quemodo Mi quodmodo Na | super] superius Se3 ‖ 9 tempus]tempore Ch *om.* CaMiRo5Se2-3SiWa | tempus imperfectum *om.* Se1 | tempus imperfectum minoris]imperfecto minoris prolationis LoNa | imperfectis CaMiSe2-3 imperfecti FaPi | minoris (*pr.*)]maioris Ro5Wa | biscantare CaChPiRo1 | deberemus]debemus FaSiWa debueritis Mi deberemus per Se2 deberetur Se3 | perfecti FaPi | minoris (*sec.*)] minorem Ca minoris prolationis Si ‖ 9–10 e converso]aequo Lo ‖ 10 sic]sic videbimus Se2 sicut Se3 | temporibus *om.* ChFa | quod]quas Na | singulariter]figuraliter LoSi figuraliter prout Ro5Wa omnibus FaNaPiRo1 *om.* Se2 ‖ 10–72.1 clare ... patebit]clare ostendere tractatum habent Ca | apparebit Wa ‖

CHAPTER TWO

ON RESTS

The rest of a duplex longa ☲ longa ☰ brevis ═ semibrevis ═ and minima ═ Of these, some perfect and some imperfect are found everywhere, just as written. Granted the masters instructed us in these noteshapes and also in the four principal mensurations (namely, in perfect tempus of major prolation and imperfect tempus of the same, and in perfect tempus of minor prolation and imperfect tempus of the same), yet they did not teach us how we ought to discant perfect tempus of minor prolation over imperfect tempus of minor prolation[6] (and conversely), and so on for the individual tempora that will clearly and individually be shown below.

---

[6]The simultaneous notation of these two mensurations is a good example of the notational need behind this treatise. The breves of perfect tempus with minor prolation and imperfect tempus with minor prolation are of differing lengths (six minimae and four minimae respectively) and so cannot be simultaneously notated with the standard *figurae*. In contrast, the combination of perfect tempus with minor prolation and imperfect tempus with major prolation is simplified, as a brevis of either mensuration is equivalent to six minimae. It is only necessary to show the basic rhythmic pattern has shifted from three groups of two to two groups of three, or conversely. The simultaneous notation of these two mensurations was codified by Philippe de Vitry in the beginning of the fourteenth century (*Philippi de Vitriaco Ars nova*, ed. Gilbert Reaney, André Gilles, and Jean Maillard, Corpus scriptorum de musica, no. 8 [(Rome): American Institute of Musicology, 1964], p. 28) by the use of red notation.

bit. Quia esset multum inconveniens quod illud quod potest pronuntiari non posset scribi et clare ostendere tractatum hunc parvulum ordinare curavi. Ac etiam que superius dixi ad effectum cum dei adiutorio producam quod intelligentibus patebit.

CAPITULUM TERTIUM

DE DIMINUTIONE FIGURARUM

Primo ostendam figuras ordinatas cum quibus diversimode discantatur non sequentes ordinem tenoris sed alterius ⟨temporis⟩ quam fuerit tenoris. Consideret ergo unusquisque per viam rationis quod omnis res plena atque perfecta si ad plenitudinem eius evacuetur non est dubium quin propter evacuationem accipit diminutionem atque imperfectionem. Verbi gratia, ‖ semi- CS3: 119b

---

1 Quia ... inconveniens]Nam esset assumendum Si Nam esset absurdum Wa Non esset assignandur Lo *om.* CaMiRo5Se1-3 | esset multum]satis Fa | inconvenienti Na | quod (*pr.*)]quia Se1-2 | illud]id Lo | potest *om.* Ca | pronuntiari]permutari Mi pronuntiari cum ore ChNaPiRo1 ‖ 1–2 inconveniens ... tractatum]inconveniens videretur illud scribere non posse quod cum ore profertur propterea tractatum Fa ‖ 2 possit Ch posse Mi potest Na Ro5Se3 | scribi]scribit Ca | et]et ut omnia Se1 et ut alia Mi et ut ergo Se3Wa et e converso quod ut clare Ro5 et ut congruit clare Lo | et clare ostendere]ut manifeste apperet clare enim ostendere Se2 | ostendere]ostendi Ro1 ostenderet Se1 ostenderem Wa ostenderunt Mi ostendere preterea NaPiRo1 | tractum Na | tractatus huius Wa | hunc]hic Na habitum Se1 | tractavi Si ‖ 2–4 Ac etiam ... patebit *om.* LoSi ‖ 3 dixi]dixit Mi *om.* Ch | perducam CaFaPiSe1-2Wa producat Se3 | quod]quod vobis Ch quod ibi CaMiSe2-3 *om.* Na ‖ 4 patebit] parebit Pi patebit et cetera Na ‖ 5 Capitulum tertium]Capitulum primum FaRo5 Capitulum secundum SiWa Capitulo tertio Mi Exemplum tertium Pi *om.* CaRo1Se1Se3 ‖ 5–6 Capitulum ... figurarum *om.* LoSe2 ‖ 6 diminutionibus Fa | figurarum]prolationum Ca figurarum et aumentationem simplicium ac compositarum Ro5Wa ‖ 7 Primo]Primum Se1Se3 Et postea Lo | signa ordinata Ca | cum *om.* Se2 | diversimodi Se3SiWa | discantatur]discantor Ch Ro5 discantur Mi discantantur PiWa potest biscantare Ca discantantur dulcimodi Lo ‖ 8 sequendo CaFaNaPiRo1Se1-2 | ordines Wa | temporis ChLo Ro5SiWa prolationis Ca *om. cett.* | quam fuerit tenoris *om.* Ca | fuerit]sit Se2 | tenoris (*sec.*)]tenor ChFaLoMiNaPiRo5Se1Si tenor tenera ratio. capitulum secundum Wa ‖ 9 Consideras Se3 Consideretur MiPi ‖ 10 perfecte Ro5 | perfecta ... evacuetur *om.* Mi | ad]ad in Se1Se3 | a plenitudine LoRo5Se2Si Wa | eius]ipsius Se1 *om.* Ch | evacuatur Ca evacuaretur Wa | est *om.* Si | dubitum ChFa | quin]quod Si ‖ 11 accipiat ChMiSiWa ‖ 11–74.1 Semibrevis perfecta *om.* Ro1 ‖

Because it would be very incongruous for that which can be performed not to be able to be written, I took care to organize this little treatise to exhibit this clearly. And as I said above, I shall bring to completion, with the help of God, what will be shown to those who understand.

CHAPTER THREE

ON THE DIMINUTION OF NOTESHAPES

First, I shall exhibit in order the noteshapes with which one discants in various ways, not following the order of the tenor but of another tempus than would be the tenor's. Let each one therefore consider, by the path of reason, that everything complete and perfect, if it should be made hollow with respect to its completeness, accepts (there is no doubt) diminution and imperfection on account of this hollowing. For example, a perfect semibre-

brevis perfecta ut hic ◆ si inventa fuerit vacua ut hic ◇ accipit diminutionem atque imperfectionem et iam perdidit tertiam partem sue virtutis quia primo valet tres minimas nunc vero valet tantum duas quod intelligentibus clarum est. Et sicut res perfecta per diminutionem imperficitur, sic simili
5 modo res imperfecta per additionem augmentatur. Verbi gratia, si brevis fuerit caudata a parte dextra superius vel inferius accipit augmentationem quod non est dubium sed est multum clarum. Et ita intendo cum dei adiutorio per augmentationem et diminutionem procedere. Et sicut ostensum est de semibreve, ita ostendam per viam evacuationem de duplici longa, de longa,
10 de breve, de semibreve et de minima.

---

1 perfecta]perfecta quia plena Fa I ◆] ◊ Ca ◆ Ro1 I si]et hec Ca sed si Se3 I si inventa fuerit vacua]si eius venter evacuetur LoRo5SiWa semibrevis imperfecta quia vacua Fa I vacua]vacua vel rubea Na *om.* Mi I ut hic (*sec.*) *om.* Fa I ◊] ◆ Ro1 II 2 atque imperfectionem *om.* Lo I imperfectionem] imperfectionem ut hic superius Ca I perdit FaNaRo5Se1Wa perdet PiRo1 I virtutis]veritatis Ca I quia]qui Na II 2–3 quin prima Ca II 3 valet (*pr.*)]valuit CaLo Si valebat ChRo5Wa I nunc ... duas]nunc autem non valet nisi duas CaRo5 Se3 nunc nullo nisi duas Ch nunc autem valet nisi duas LoWa nunc autem nolo valet nisi duas Si I vero valet]solum Fa I valet (*sec.*) *om.* Fa I tantum *om.* Mi I quod]et de istis Ca II 4 clarum est]datur Lo clarum est. Et minima etiam si evacuetur similiter perdit tertiam partem sue virtutis. Si I sicut]sic FaSe1Si sed Lo si Se3 *om.* Ro5 I perfectam Fa I imperficit Ca I sic *om.* Mi I simili]scilicet Lo II 5 imperfectam Fa I adiectionem Ro1Se1Se3(?) augmentationem Ca II 6 dextera PiRo1Ro5 I inferius]inferius tunc Ca I augmentationem atque diminutionem Ch II 7 dubitum Ch I est (*sec.*) *om.* FaLoRo1Ro5Si Wa I multum clarum. Et sic res perfecta per diminutionem imperficitur sic simili modo res imperfecta per additionem augmentatur. Et ita intendo ... Fa I ita *om.* Ro1 II 8 sicut]id Lo sic Mi I est]fuerit Lo fuit Si II 9 semibrevi FaMi PiRo1Ro5Se3 breve Ca semibrevi et de minima Si I per viam *om.* Na I viam *om.* Si I evacuationis FaPiRo1Wa evacuationis ut Lo I non de duplici longa *in marg.* Fa I de longa *om.* ChMiSe3 II 10 breve]brevi MiRo5Se3 brevi et adhuc etiam Si brevis CaNa I semibreve]semibrevi MiRo5Se3 semibrevis CaNa *om.* Se1 II

vis, as here ✦ if it should be found hollow, as here ✧ accepts diminution and imperfection and now has lost a third part of its force because first it was worth three minimae but now is worth only two, which is clear to those who understand. And, as a perfect thing is imperfected through diminution, thus in a similar manner an imperfect thing is augmented through addition. For example, if a tail is added to a brevis on the right side, either above or below, it accepts augmentation; on that, there is no doubt—it is very clear. And so, with the help of God, I intend to proceed through augmentation and diminution. And just as was exhibited for the semibrevis, I shall exhibit for the duplex longa, longa, brevis, semibrevis, and minima by the path of hollowing out.

CAPITULUM QUARTUM

DE EVACUATIONE FIGURARUM

    Duplex longa de modo perfecto de eius proprietate valet sex tempora, et si evacuetur amittit tertiam partem sue virtutis quemadmodum semibrevis ut
5 superius dictum est et valet quatuor temporum ut hic ⊓̣

    Item longa perfecta que de sua proprietate valet tria tempora, si evacuetur amittit tertiam partem sue virtutis et non valet nisi duo tempora ut hic ⊓̣

    ‖ Item brevis perfecta que de sua proprietate valet tres semibreves, si evacuetur amittit tertiam partem sue virtutis et non valet nisi duas semibreves ut   CS3:
10 hic ◼   120a

    Item semibrevis perfecta que de sua proprietate valet tres minimas, si evacuetur amittit tertiam partem sue virtutis et non valet nisi duas minimas ut hic ◆

    Minima similiter si evacuetur merito etiam debet perdere tertiam partem
15 sue virtutis et de eius valore infra declarabo.

1–2 Capitulum ... figurarum *om.* CaFaLoMiNaPiRo1Ro5Se1Se3SiWa ‖ 3 Duplex]Duplex ergo FaNaPiRo1Se1 Duplex est Ro5 ǀ Duplex longa de] Duplex quando ammictis sicut de Se3 ǀ longa]longa que sit CaLoMiRo5 longa que fit Wa ǀ de eius proprietate *om.* Ch ǀ eius]eiusdem Se3 cuius NaWa ǀ valet]videlicet Pi ǀ sex]novem Ro5Wa ǀ tempora]tempora sive breves Ro1 ‖ 3–4 et si]si autem Si ‖ 4 evacuata fuerit Ca ǀ amittit *om.* Se3 ǀ virtutis]valoris Ca temporis vel virtutis Ro5 ǀ ut]de qua NaPiRo1Se1 *om.* LoRo5Si ‖ 4–5 ut superius dictum est *om.* Fa ‖ 5 superius]super Ca superius iam CaMiSe3Si ǀ dictum]dixi Se1 dicta Ro5SiWa ante dicta Lo ǀ est *om.* Ro5SiWa ǀ et]et tunc Ch ǀ et valet]tunc facta est LoRo5SiWa sic erit Fa et est PiRo1Se1 *om.* CaMi Se3 ǀ quatuor]sex Ro5Wa ǀ tempora ChPiRo5Se3 ‖ 6 que]quando Se3 ǀ de *om.* Mi ǀ sue Ca ǀ propriete Fa ‖ 7 amittet Fa amittat Lo ǀ non *om.* FaLoNaPi Ro1 ǀ nisi *om.* FaNaPiRo1 ǀ duo tempora]dua tempora Se3 duas Mi ‖ 8 Item *om.* Ro5 ǀ que]quando Se3 ‖ 8–10 Item ... nisi duas semibreves ut hic *om.* Mi ‖ 8–9 evacuatur Ca ‖ 9 amittit]amittat Lo *om.* Ca ǀ sue virtutis *om.* LoRo5 ǀ non *om.* FaLoNaPiRo1 ǀ nisi *om.* FaNaPiRo1 ǀ semibreves *om.* FaNaPiSe1 ‖ 11 Item *om.* Ro5 ǀ que de sua proprietate *om.* Ro1 ǀ de *om.* Mi ǀ tres minimas sed si Wa ‖ 12 evacuatur Mi ǀ amittat Lo ǀ amittit ... sue virtutis *om.* Fa PiRo1 ǀ non *om.* FaLoNaPiRo1 ǀ nisi *om.* FaNaPiRo1 ǀ minimas *om.* FaMiPi Se1 ‖ 12–15 evacuetur ... declarabo]evacuetur merito etiam debet perdere tertiam partem sue virtutis et de eius valore inferius declarabo Na evacuetur tertiam partem sue virtutis et de eius valore inferius declarabo Ca ‖ 14 non hic Bonadies *in marg.* Fa ǀ Minima]Item minima Fa Omnia Mi ǀ similiter]etiam LoSe1 ǀ evacuatur Se3 ǀ merito etiam debet perdere]amittere Ch ‖ 15 et]sed LoSiWa ǀ eius]istis Mi ǀ inferius ChLoMiRo5Se3SiWa ǀ declarando Mi ǀ ♩ *add.* ChPi ut hic ♩ ♪ ♪ *add.* Fa sub hac forma ut hic patet *add.* Ro5 sub hac figura ut hic patet *add.* Wa ‖

CHAPTER FOUR

ON THE HOLLOWING OUT OF NOTESHAPES

A duplex longa of perfect modus in accordance with its propriety contains six tempora, and if hollowed out, it gives up a third of its force in the same way as the semibrevis (as stated above) and is worth four tempora, as here

A perfect longa, which in accordance with its propriety is worth three tempora, if hollowed out gives up a third part of its force and is worth only two tempora, as here

A perfect brevis, which in accordance with its propriety is worth three semibreves, if hollowed out gives up a third part of its force and is worth only two semibreves, as here

A perfect semibrevis, which in accordance with its propriety is worth three minimae, if hollowed out gives up a third part of its force and is worth only two minimae, as here

Similarly, a minima, if hollowed out, ought also to lose a third part of its force by merit, and I shall make clear its value below.

Item punctus perfectionis, si vacuus fuerit, accipit diminutionem per dimidietatem et non per tertiam quia nichil habet sub se, id est nullam figuram sicut alie figure iam dicte. Et sic numerando minus corpus dividitur in duas partes et est minor prolatio que potest fieri, id est in duas semiminimas
5 quando est in minori valore, id est quod valet minimam, sicut puncto quia aliquando valet brevem, aliquando semibrevem et aliquando minimam. Et tunc dividendo in duas partes id est evacuando punctum valet tantum quantum una pars minime divise in duas partes; id est semiminima ut hic °. Et isti duo tunc faciunt minimam ut hic °°.

---

1 punctus *om.* Na | vacuum Ca evacuatus Wa | si vacuus fuerit]si evacuetur Na si evacuetur vel vacuus fuerit Ro1 si vacuus fuerit°Mi || 2 medietatem CaRo5Se3 dimidiam partem FaNaPiRo1Se1 | per *om.* Lo | tertiam partem CaChLoMiRo5Si | quia]quod Ca | nichil]nec Lo nisi Wa | habet *om.* Lo | id est]et Ca || 2–3 nulla figura Se3 || 3 sicut]sed Lo | sicut alie figure *om.* Se3 | alia figura Lo | iam dicte]predicte FaNaPiRo1Se1 *om.* Ch | iam dicte et sic numerandus est. Minor corpus Mi | Et sicut minima dum est minor corpus ChRo5SiWa Et sed minima dum est unus corpus (?) Lo Et sic numerandum est que minor corpus Ca | numerando est Se3 | minor CaChFaMiRo5Se3Si Wa | dividet Wa dividi Ca || 4 minoris prolationis Se3 | que]quod PiRo5 | id est]etiam Mi *om.* Ro1Se3 | minimas NaRo1Se1 || 4–9 partes ... ut hic]partes equales videlicet semiminimam quam due in minori prolatione faciunt unam minimam Ca || 5 quando]que Na tamen Se3 | minori]minor Na minimari Se3 | valore *om.* NaRo1Se1 | id est ... puncto]id est minima valet punctum valet minimam FaPi | quod]que Na quando ChMiSi | minimam]minima ChRo5 Se3Wa *om.* LoSi | sicut]sic ChLo sic cum Ro5 | sicut puncto]si per punctum Se3 *om.* FaNaRo1Se1 | punctus Wa | quia]quoniam Pi || 5–6 quia aliquando] quondam aliis Fa || 6 aliquando (*pr.*)]autem Lo | brevem]brevialem Lo brevem vel brevialem Ro5 | aliquando (*sec.*) *om.* LoSi | aliquando semibrevem *om.* Mi | et ... minimam]et ante minimam Lo || 6–7 Et tunc *om.* Lo | Et tunc potest dividi ChRo5Wa | Et quando valet minimam potest dividi in duas partes equales et evacuare punctum Si || 7 potest dividi Lo | dividitur MiSe3 | id est *om.* LoNaSi | evacuare punctum LoMiRo5SiWa evacuatur punctus Se3 | punctum tunc ChLoMiSe3SiWa | valet]naturalem Ro1 || 7–8 quantum] sicut ChMiRo5Se3SiWa sed Lo || 8 divise id est Ro5 | in duas *om.* Se1 | partes equales Si | id est]in NaMi | semiminimam FaMiPiRo1Wa | ut hic et cetera Na | ⸲ₒ *add.* Fa || 8–9 Et isti ... ut hic *om.* ChMi || 9 tunc]autem Fa tantum Si | ut hic apparet Ro5 ut hic et cetera Na | °°.°° *add.* Se1 ₒₒ⸲ *add.* FaSi ||

The dot of perfection,⁷ if made hollow, accepts diminution by half and not by a third because there is nothing beneath it, that is, no noteshape like the other noteshapes already mentioned. And as, by reckoning, a smaller body is divided into two parts and is the smaller prolation that can be made—that is, into two semiminimae when this is applied to the smaller value, that is, what is worth a minima—so it is with the dot, because sometimes it is worth a brevis, sometimes a semibrevis, and sometimes a minima. And then, by dividing it into two parts—that is, by hollowing out the dot—, it is worth one part of a minima that has been divided in two—that is, a semiminima—, as here ∘.⁸ And these two, then, make a minima, as here ∘∘.

---

⁷This is one of the most confusing portions of the *Tractatus figurarum*, as is shown by the number of variants in the surviving sources. The author's argument is that the dot of perfection varies in duration (even though it has only one shape) as its value is determined by the note to which it is affixed. The smallest *figura* to which it is attached is the semibrevis, in which case the dot is worth a minima. It is this particular dot that is made hollow, and as the minima is immensurable, so is this dot. Thus, when made hollow, it is worth a semiminima.

⁸The hollow dot does not appear in any surviving music. It does appear, however, in a reworking of Boen's treatise contained in a manuscript of Italian provenance written sometime after 1375 (*Ars [musicae]* [ed. Gallo], pp. 12–14).

CAPITULUM QUINTUM

DE AUGMENTATIONE FIGURARUM

Nunc videndum est de augmentatione figurarum. Et considero tamen non fore necesse gra‖datim descendere de augmentatione sicut de diminu-   CS3:
5 tione, videlicet de duplici longa vel etiam longa, sed tantummodo de breve   120b
et infra, quia esset quedam dilatio vel evasio si cantor plus requiesceret se
quam super brevem. Et primo volo dicere de semiminima quia sine ipsa factum est nichil in musica. Et licet aliqui magistri dicunt quod non est dare
ultra minimam, quod ego teneo, tamen oportet quod per signa cognoscantur
10 qualitates ipsarum figurarum. Verbi gratia, si longa et brevis ligate sunt ut
hic ♦ apponendo proprietatem efficientur id quod vis, quod si proprietas a
parte sinistra inferiori descendat fient ambe breves ut hic ♦ quod si a parte

---

1 Capitulum quintum *om.* CaMiNaRo1Se1Se3 Capitulum secundum FaRo5 Exemplum quartum capitulo duo Pi Capitulum tertium SiWa ‖ 1–2 Capitulum … figurarum *om.* Lo ‖ 2 diminutione Si ǀ figurarum *om.* CaWa ‖ 3 de augmentatione figurarum *om.* Se3 ǀ consideram Se3 ǀ tamen]tantum Ca ‖ 4 non]nunc Mi *om.* Ca ǀ necessarium Ca ǀ gradatim]tradatim Na gradatim in ChLoSe3 gradatim inde Si ǀ descendere]dicere FaNaPiRo1Se1 ǀ sicut]sive Ch sic Na sed Lo ‖ 5 dupla Ch ǀ vel etiam]et FaNaPiRo1 ǀ vel etiam longa *om.* Se1 ǀ etiam]etiam de Ro5 ǀ tantummodo]tantum Si tamen modo Na tamen de modo Ca ǀ brevi FaMiPiRo1Ro5Se3SiWa ‖ 6 infra]ista Ro1 ita Fa NaPi ǀ esset *om.* LoWa ǀ quidam Mi ǀ dilatio]dilacetatio Ro5 delaceratio Wa delatio FaPi ǀ vel evasio *om.* FaNaPiRo1Se1 ǀ evasio]evasio quod ChLoMi Se3 invasio quod Ca ǀ sicut Fa ǀ canto Mi ǀ requiesceret]requiescet Lo quiescerit Fa quiesceret PiRo1Se1 ǀ se]se plus Ro5 *om.* NaRo1Se1 ‖ 7 Et primo] De semiminima *add. ante* Wa Postea Lo ǀ volo]intendo CaFaNaPiRo1 ‖ 7–8 Et primo … nichil in musica *om.* Ca ‖ 8 est (*pr.*)]esset SiWa ǀ in musica *om.* Se3 ǀ Et licet aliqui]Et licet quod Si *om.* Ca ǀ alii Na ǀ magistri *om.* Ro1 ǀ magister dicit Ca ǀ dicunt]dicant FaLoMiPiSe1Si *om.* Na ǀ dare *om.* Se3 ‖ 9 ego]ego etiam LoRo5SiWa ǀ tamen]tunc Ca ǀ oportet]oppositum Se1 ǀ signa]signam Ro5 signa figuram Wa ǀ cognoscuntur CaChFaNa ‖ 10 qualitatem Na ǀ ligatur Si longata Na ǀ ligatura sint Lo ǀ sint ChMiWa ‖ 10–11 ut hic *om.* Fa ‖ 11 *fig. vac. et pl.* Fa *vac.* CaSe3 ǀ imponendo Si ǀ proprietates Wa proprietate Na ǀ efficiuntur FaMiNaPiRo1 efficiunt Ca ǀ id quod]eodem modo sicut Ch id quod si Wa ǀ id quod vis *om.* Ca ǀ quod (*pr.*)]ad que Na ‖ 11–12 apponendo … breves ut hic *om.* Se3 ‖ 12 inferiori *om.* Ro5 ǀ descendentur Ch descendatur Ca ǀ fiant FaNaPiSe1 ǀ ambe]ambo Na due Ro5Wa enim Ch ambe tunc Se3 tunc LoSi ǀ ambe breves *om.* Ca ǀ breves ut supra Fa ǀ quod]et Ro5 *om.* Na ‖ 12–82.1 quod si … ambe semibreves ut hic *om.* Ca ‖

CHAPTER FIVE

ON THE AUGMENTATION OF NOTESHAPES

Now must be seen the augmentation of noteshapes. I do not consider it to be necessary, however, to descend step-by-step through augmentation as I did through diminution, namely, through the duplex longa or longa, but only through the brevis and below, because there would be a certain delay or evasion if a singer would rest longer than a brevis. And first, I wish to speak of the semiminima because no music is made without it. Granted, some masters say that there is nothing smaller than a minima (something which I myself believe), yet it is neccessary that the qualities of the noteshapes themselves be recognized through signs. For example, if a longa and a brevis are bound together as here ◥ then by applying propriety, they will accomplish what you wish: if propriety descends from the left side, both become breves, as here ◤ ; or if it ascends from the left side, both become semibreves, as

sinistra superiori ascendat fient ambe semibreves ut hic ♩ et sic de aliis. Sic et nunc minime plene vel vacue aliquando per signum et aliquando per proprietatem suscipiunt diminutionem vel augmentationem sicut inferius patebit. Et hec est que vocatur semiminima ♪ et due istarum valent unam
5 minimam. Et minor prolatio non potest fieri si recte consideras. Et ista adiuncta aliis figuris dat augmentationem taliter quod diversimode potest discantari et hoc alio modo quam sit tenor.

CAPITULUM SEXTUM

DE AUGMENTATIONE ET DIMINUTIONE FIGURARUM

10 Brevis autem que perdidit tertiam partem sue virtutis ponuntur ex illis tres pro duobus temporibus perfecti maioris ut hic ▫▫▫ . Potest autem tempus dividi in duas partes equales ut hic ♦·♦·

quia semibreves perfecte atque punctate valent quelibet quatuor minimas, et

---

1 sinistra *om.* CaFaNaPiRo1 | superiori]superior ChFaSe1 *om.* Ro5 | ascendat] ascendant ChLo ascendet Ro1 descendat Mi | fiant FaPiSe1 | ambe]due Ro5 ambe tunc Se3 tunc LoMiSi *om.* Ch | et sic de aliis *om.* Fa || 2 Sic]Sicut Ro5SiWa Sed Lo *om.* Ch | nunc *om.* Ca | minores Ca | plene aut vacue FaPi vel plene aut vacue Ro1 vel plene aut rubee vel vacue Na | aliquando per (*sec.*) *om.* Ca | per (*sec.*) *om.* Se1Wa || 3 diminutionem *om.* Mi | vel]ut Fa | sicut]sic CaNa sed Lo || 4 patebunt Ca | hoc Fa | est *om.* Se3 | quod Ca | que vocatur *om.* NaRo1Se1 | semiminimam Se3 semiminima ut hic Ca | ♪ ChSi ♪ PiSe1Wa ○ Ro1 ♪♪♪ Fa ▫♪ Na | unam *om.* CaChFa || 5 minimam ut hic ♪♪♪ Ca | Et quia Ch Et credo quod LoRo5SiWa Et quod CaMi | maior Fa | possit LoWa | consideres Ch | ista]istam Mi illa Na ita Lo || 5–6 adiuncta]adiuta Ca addita Ch adiuncta ad Na adiunctionem Mi || 6 dant PiRo1Se1 | taliter]talem LoRo5Wa taliter pro Se3 | diversimodi Se3Si dulcimodi Lo | possunt Lo || 6–7 discantari]cantari FaNaRo1 cantare Pi biscantari Ca || 7 hoc]hec Se3 hoc est LoSe1 *om.* Wa | quam]quod Se3 quam non PiRo1 | sit *om.* Si | tenor et cetera Na || 8 Capitulum sextum *om.* MiNaRo1Se1Se3Wa Capitulo tertio Pi Capitulum tertium Fa Capitulum quartum Si || 8–9 Capitulum ... figurarum *om.* CaLoRo5 || 9 Item de augmentatione MiNaSe1Si Wa | et de Ch | figurarum *om.* FaNaPiRo1 || 10 De brevibus autem quarum quelibet perdit tertiam FaNaPiRo1Se1 | autem *om.* Mi | que]quod Se3 | perdidit]reddidit Ch perdit Si | sue virtutis *om.* FaNaPiRo1Se1 | ponitur MiNa | ex illis *om.* FaNaPiRo1Se1 | illis]istis Ca || 11 tribus CaMi | duabus brevibus sive Ro1 | perfectis LoSiWa | minoris Ca | autem]aliter Se3 autem istud Si || 11–12 tempus]tempore Ch tempora Se3 *om.* FaPi || 12 ut hic *om.* Ca | hic]sic MiRo1 | ♦·♦· Se1 ♦♦♦♦ Ro5 ♦♦ Ro1 ♦·♦· FaPi ♦♦ vel ♦·♦· vel ♦·♦· Si ♦·♦·♦♦ Wa ♦♦ Na ◊ ◊ Ca ♦·♦· Lo || 14 quia]super per Fa | quia semibrevis perfecta Ca | semibrevis Ch || 14–84.1 quelibet quatuor ... valent *om.* Lo ||

here ♩ ; and so on for the others. Likewise, filled or hollow minimae receive diminution or augmentation, sometimes by a sign or sometimes by propriety, as will be shown below. This is what is called a semiminima ♪ [9] and two of them are worth one minima. A smaller prolation cannot be made, if you consider it rightly. And this added to other noteshapes gives augmentation in such a way that it can be discanted in various manners and another mode than the tenor would be.[10]

CHAPTER SIX

ON THE AUGMENTATION AND DIMINUTION OF NOTESHAPES[11]

A brevis that has lost a third part of its force: there are placed three of these for two tempora of perfect tempus of major prolation, as here ▫▫▫ . It is also possible to divide the tempus into two equal parts, as here ♪·♪· because semibreves that are perfect and dotted are each worth four minimae[12] and the additions to them are each worth a semiminima, and so these

---

[9] The *figura* of the semiminima varied throughout the fourteenth century. A notable feature of the author's chosen form is that it is hollow. Most likely this was done to differentiate it from the filled semiminima, which he calls an imperfect minima, four of which are equivalent to three minimae (cf. chapt. 6 [pp. 84–85]).

[10] The semiminima is an integral part of the author's system, although it never appears as an independent *figura*. It is combined with two dotted, perfect semibreves (cf. n. 12) to change the tempus from perfect to imperfect in perfect tempus with major prolation (cf. chapt. 7 [pp. 88–93]) and two minimae to change the prolation from major to minor (cf. chapts. 7–8).

[11] From the patterns developed in this chapter, it is clear the author is attempting to create traditional rhythmic patterns that will imply a mensuration other than the tenor's. He does not appear interested in the *figurae* for their abstract rhythmic value and their use to create complex rhythms without out mensural implications.

[12] Another peculiarity of the author's system is the anomalous use of a dot of addition with an already perfect note, in this case a semibrevis. As this concept is used nowhere else in the *Tractatus* and is never presented formally in the introductory chapters, its use appears to be purely expedient. There would be no other way of creating the proportion two in the time of nine with the given *figurae*.

sibi adiuncte valent ‖ quelibet seminimimam et iste due figure perficiunt   CS3:
novem minimas.   121a
   Item semibrevis imperfecta perficitur per punctum ut hic ◆·◆·
   Item minima caudata superius et inferius valet tantum quantum semibre-
5 vis imperfecta, id est duas minimas, et hoc satis commune ut hic

   Abstrahe autem a qualibet tertiam partem id est evacua, et invenies quatuor minimas si recte computes ut hic

10 et sic iste tres valent quatuor minimas.
   Sunt autem et alie figure que vocantur minime imperfecte ex quibus
ponuntur quatuor pro tribus minimis. Et habent maiorem effectum quam
semiminime quia sunt plene, et habent minorem effectum quam minime
quia habent signum atque proprietatem semiminime ut hic
15

---

1 sibi]si Si ǀ adiuta qualibet semiminima Ca ǀ adiuncte]ad invicem Wa ǀ quelibet *om*. FaNaPiRo1 ǀ et tunc FaNaPiRo1 ǀ iste]ille Na ǀ due]quatuor Ro5Wa
ǀ figure *om*. Ca ‖ 1–2 adjuncte … novem]adiuncte fuerint caude semiminimarum novem minimas quia quelibet valet quatuor minimas et semiminimam et sic sunt novem Si ‖ 2 novem minimas ut hic ◆·◆· Fa ‖ 3 Item …
per punctum ut hic *om*. Mi ǀ imperfecta *om*. Si ǀ perficit Ca ǀ ut hic apparet
Ro5 ǀ ◆◆ Ro1 ◇·◇· CaFaLo ‖ 4 et *om*. LoNa ǀ tantum]tamen MiNa ǀ
quantum]tantum Ca ‖ 5 imperfectam Ca ǀ id est]ut in Ca ǀ et hoc]ut hic Fa ǀ et
hoc satis commune *om*. Lo ǀ hoc est CaRo1 ǀ commune]convenientur Wa ǀ
commune est ChSi *om*. Mi ǀ ut hic apparet Ro5 ǀ ut hic *om*. Na ‖ 6
 Ca Lo ǀ non hic *in mar*. Fa ‖ 7 Abstraha Ch Extrahe FaNaPi
Ro1Se1 ǀ autem *om*. Ca ǀ a *om*. Fa ǀ quelibet FaRo5 ǀ evacua]evacuata Ca
evacue Ro5 caudata Se3 ǀ inveniens Na ‖ 8 minimas sic Si ǀ si bene numeres
ut hic FaNaRo1 si bene numeras ut hic Pi ǀ computas Ro5Se1Se3 ǀ ut hic *om*.
Si ‖ 9 vel ◇◇◇ *in marg*. Se1 Lo *om*. Ca ‖ 10 sic]si CaSe3 *om*. Ro1 ǀ iste
om. Ca ‖ 11 autem *om*. Se3 ǀ et]ut Se3 ǀ figurarum Si ǀ que vocantur *om*. Wa ǀ
ex quibus *om*. Se3 ‖ 12 ponuntur]ponitur MiNa *om*. Fa ǀ minimis]minimas
FaSe3 *om*. Pi ‖ 13 semiminimas Si semiminima Lo ǀ semiminime quia …
quam *om*. MiSe3 ǀ quia *om*. Se3 ǀ maiorum FaPi ǀ minima Lo ‖ 14 signum]
figuram Pi ǀ atque]seu CaSe3 ǀ semiminimarum Ro5Wa ‖ 15 Se3
Ro1 Ca ‖

two noteshapes complete nine minimae.¹³

An imperfect semibrevis is perfected by the dot, as here ◆·◆·

A minima to which a tail has been added both above and below is worth as much as an imperfect semibrevis, that is, two minimae, and this is rather common, as here ↕↕↕ ¹⁴

Take from them a third part of each, that is, hollow them out, and you will discover four minimae if you count correctly, as here ⦵⦵⦵

and thus these three are worth four minimae.

There are other noteshapes that are called imperfect minimae,¹⁵ four of which are placed for three minimae. They have a greater effect than semiminimae because they are filled and have a lesser effect than minimae because they have the sign and propriety of semiminimae, as here ♪♪♪♪

---

¹³This is the first example of a composite *figura*. It is created through the physical combination of a dotted perfect semibrevis (equivalent to four minimae, cf. n. 12) and a semiminima (equivalent to half a minima). The resultant *figura* is equivalent to four-and-a-half minimae.

¹⁴Another composite *figura*. Each noteshape is the physical combination of two minimae into one *figura* and is therefore equivalent to two minimae. A *figura* with an identical form is the *fusa* (cf. Oliver B. Ellsworth, ed., *The Berkeley Manuscript*, Greek and Latin Music Theory, vol. 2 [Lincoln: University of Nebraska Press, 1984], p. 126); this *figura* is created through the addition of a descending tail to a minima and is equivalent to one-and-a-half minimae. The parallel *figura* in the author's system is discussed in chapt. 6.

¹⁵These *figurae* are necessary in order to create the proportion 4:3. They appear in other theorists' writings as well under the name of *additae* (cf. *Berkeley Manuscript* [ed. Ellsworth], p. 124).

Possunt autem aliquando poni rubee figure diversimode figurate. Et quando homo non habet cum quo possit scribere rubeas figuras, tunc est licitum ipsas evacuare. Sed hoc est tantum de tempore imperfecto maioris prolationis super tempus perfectum minoris prolationis et e converso.

5 Item figure superius et inferius caudate vel cauda inferius retorta, quatuor ex istis valent septem minimas ut hic

Quod si adiungatur eis punctus vacuus qui valet tantum quantum semiminima, tunc iste ‖ quatuor valent novem minimas si recte computes ut hic

CS3: 121b

---

1 Posset Si | autem om. Na | aliquando]aliis Fa | poni om. Lo | figure] similiter Wa | diversimodi LoSe3Si | figurate]figurare Ro5Se3 figurarum LoSi om. Ca | Et]Et hoc Ch Videlicet Ca ‖ 2 homo]hoc Lo aliquis homo Si | habet] haberet Wa potest Se3 | cum quo]unde NaPiRo1 om. FaMi | possit]posset LoSe1 om. ChMiNaRo5Wa | possit scribere]ad scribendum Mi | scribere] scribat Ch scriberet Wa scribere potest Se3 | rubeis figuris Lo | tunc om. Ca | est om. Si | tunc est]et non est Lo ‖ 2–3 lictum CaChFaWa licet Si ‖ 3 evacuari Ca vacuare ChLoRo1Se1 vacare NaSe3 | Sed]Et NaSi | hoc est om. Ca | tantum]tunc Na | de om. Fa | maiori Wa ‖ 3–4 maioris prolationis om. Ca ‖ 4 prolationis (pr.) om. ChMiRo5Se1Se3SiWa | super]sicut Na | perfectum om. NaRo1Se1 | minorem Ch | prolationis (sec.) om. ChNaRo1Si | et]vel Mi | e converso] modo Ch aequo Lo ‖ 5 figure]figura LoMiPiRo5Se1SiWa figure diversimode Ca | caudate]caudata LoMiPiRo5Se1SiWa caudatur Ca | vel]si Mi | vel ... retorta]cuius cauda inferius est retorta LoRo5SiWa et retorta Ca | cauda]caude FaNaPiRo1 | retorta]retorte FaNaPiRo1 ‖ 6 ex istis] existentes Ro1 | istis]illis CaLo | septem]sex Ro1Ro5SiWa ‖ 7 Se3 Ca Lo ‖ 8 Quod]Et Se3 | adiungatur]adiungitur ChMi ammictantur Se3 augmentatur Ca | eis om. CaFaNaMiPiRo1Se1Se3 | punctus vacuus]per punctum vacuum CaSe3 | qui om. Na | valet]valet qualibet Ca | tantum] tamen Na | quantum]quam Lo ‖ 8–9 qui ... semiminima]quia semiminima Se3 ‖ 9 tunc om. Na | iste]ille LoNa | si recte computes om. Lo | recte]bene FaNa PiRo1 | computas Ro5Se1Wa | computas ut hic Se3 ‖ 10 Ro5Se3 Ro1 Ca Lo ‖

Sometimes red noteshapes formed in various ways can be placed. When a man does not have anything with which he can write red noteshapes, then it is permissible to hollow them out. But this notation is only used for imperfect tempus of major prolation over perfect tempus of minor prolation (and conversely).[16]

Four noteshapes with a tail above and below and with the lower tail turned back on itself are worth seven minimae, as here  [17]

If a hollow dot, which is worth as much as a semiminima, is added to them, then those four are worth nine minimae, if you count correctly, as here

---

[16]The author's use of red notation is not entirely clear. He does wish to limit its use to the simultaneous notation of perfect tempus with minor prolation and imperfect tempus with major prolation as established by Philippe de Vitry. His examples in chapters 8 and 9, however, imply an even more limited usage, for red notation is used in situations in which it does not affect the duration of the *figurae*. When it is necessary to show a change of duration, the author prefers to use the dot of addition (chapt. 9 [pp. 97–98]) or void notation (chapt. 8 [pp. 94–95]). By keeping these two concepts separate (that is, allowing red notation to be only a sign of imperfection, not a cause), the author eliminates an element of confusion in the notation of this time.

[17]Another example of composite *figurae*. In this case, four minimae are physically combined with four imperfect minimae to create four *figurae* equivalent to seven minimae. When a hollow dot is added to each of the above *figurae*, the resultant group (cf. *infra*) is equivalent to nine minimae and is used to imply imperfect tempus with minor prolation while in perfect tempus with major prolation (cf. chapt. 7 [pp. 90–91]).

Item minima superius semiplena et inferius semivacua in uno corpore superius et inferius caudata et inferius retorta valet minimam cum semiminima ut hic ♪♪

5 quia superius sunt figure minime et inferius semiminime.

Item minima evacuata amittit tertiam partem sue virtutis ut superius dixi et sic tales tres faciunt duas minimas ut hic ♪♪♪

CAPITULUM SEPTIMUM

10   QUALITER IPSAS FIGURAS ORDINABIS PRO TEMPORIBUS

De tempore perfecto maioris prolationis.

Superius dictum est de diminutione atque augmentatione figurarum, nunc ostendam qualiter ipsas ordinabis pro temporibus. Et primo de tempore per-

---

1 minima]semiminima Se1 *om.* Se3 | superius *om.* Na | in uno corpore]in parte NaRo1 *om.* MiSe1Se3 | uno *om.* CaChFaPi | corpore]tempore Lo || 1–2 uno corpore et in parte inferius cauda retorta FaPi || 1–3 semivacua ... semiminima]semivacua et inferius in corpore caudata valet tres minimas cum semiminima Ca || 2 superius *om.* CaMiNa | superius ... caudata *om.* ChNa Ro1Se3 | et inferius retorta *om.* LoMiNaSe1Se3Si | inferius (*sec.*)]inferiori Ch | valet]videlicet Na valet tres Ca || 4 ♪♪ Se3 ♪♪ Pi ♪♪ vel ♪♪ Si ♪♪ Ca ♪♪ (?) Lo || 5 sint Ca | figure *om.* CaRo5Wa | minime]nunc Ca | et inferius sunt ChSe3 || 6 Iterum Se3 | vacuata Ca | partem *om.* Na | virtutem Ro1 | ut]sicut LoRo5SiWa *om.* Se3 || 7 sicut Ca | duas minimas ut superius dictum est de diminutione atque augmentatione figurare Ca | ut hic]ut hic et cetera Na *om.* Fa || 8 ♪♪♪ ♪♪ FaSe3 *om.* Ca || 9–11 Capitulum septimum]Capitulum tertium qualiter ordinabis et discantabis ponendo figuras de uno modo ad alium Ro5Wa || 9–10 Capitulum ... pro temporibus *om.* CaFa MiNaPiRo1Se1Se3 | De ordinatione figurarum super quatuor tempora LoSi || 10 temporibus supra tenorum Ch || 11 Et primo de tempore Si | Et postea de tempore Lo | De tempore ... prolationis *om.* CaChMiRo5Se1Se3Wa | prolationis *om.* NaSi || 12 Superius dictum est ... figurarum *om.* Ca | est *om.* Mi | figurarum]figurare Ca *om.* Lo || 12–13 Superius ... ordinabis pro temporibus *om.* Ch || 13 ostendam]ostendum Ro5 ostendam vobis Se1 | ipsas]istas Lo | ordinabimus Ca | primo]postea Lo | ☉ *in marg.* Na ||

A minima half-filled above and half-empty below in one body—and with a tail above and below and with the lower tail turned back on itself—is worth a minima and a semiminima, as here [figure] ¹⁸

because above are the noteshapes of minimae and below of semiminimae.

A minima hollowed out gives up a third part of its force as I said above, and thus three such minimae make two, as here [figure] ¹⁹

CHAPTER SEVEN

HOW YOU WILL ARRANGE THESE SAME NOTESHAPES IN THE TEMPORA

On perfect tempus of major prolation.

I spoke above concerning the diminution and augmentation of noteshapes; now I shall exhibit how you will order these same noteshapes in the tempora. First, on perfect tempus of major prolation: if we wish to discant

---

[18]The last example of a composite *figura*. In this case, the physical combination of a minima and a semiminima. Two of these *figurae* are used to replace three minimae and are equivalent in function to the *fusa* (cf. n. 14).

[19]For a discussion of the implications of the use of void minimae, see the Introduction, pp. 15–19.

fecto maioris prolationis quod si super ipsum discantare volumus ad modum imperfecti temporis minoris, appone tales quatuor figuras

|| Item si ad modum temporis imperfecti maioris dividendo tempus in duas partes appone has figuras

Item si vis dividere duo tempora istius temporis perfecti in tres partes equales appone istas figuras . Item si secundum eundem actum iterum temporis perfecti maioris vis dividere in quatuor partes appone has figuras

CS3: 122a

---

1 prolationis *om.* Ro5SiWa | quod]ut LoSi | si *om.* Na | ipsius Mi | biscantare Ca | volumus]velomus Pi velimus Fa volueris LoSi || 2 imperfecti] imperfectum ChRo5Se3Wa perfectum Ca | temporis *om.* MiSi | minoris]maioris Lo Se3 minoris prolationis CaCh | C *in marg.* Na | figuris ut hic CaFaNa || 3 ChNaSe1Se3Si Ro5 FaPiRo1Wa Ca Lo || 4 si]si vis Se3 *om.* Ca | C *in marg.* Na | ad]de Lo | perfecti CaChSe3Si | dividendo]ad dividendum Se1 divide modo Lo | tempus]tempore ChSe3 tempora Ro1 || 4–5 Item … has figuras *om.* Mi || 5 has] tales LoSi || 6 NaSe1(*sine punc.*)Se3(*punc. vac.*) (?) Ro5Wa FaPiRo1 Si Ca Lo || 7 dividere]discantare LoSi | dua Se3 due Mi | istius]ipsius Se3 | perfecti]imperfecti CaLo perfecti maioris Ch | tres *om.* Ro5 || 8 aponendo Mi | istas]has CaCh | figuras *om.* Se3 | figuras ut hic FaNa | iterum]item Se3 *om.* Si || 8–9 Item … in *om.* Ca || 9 tempus NaSe3 | tempus perfectum FaPiRo1Se1 | perfecti]imperfecti LoRo5Se3Wa | perfecti maioris discantare et dividere Si | vis *om.* Se3 | vis dividere]vis videre dividere Ro5 *om.* FaNaPi | partes non equales Si | apponens Mi | has] tales Ro5SiWa | has figuras]tales Lo | figuras ut hic FaRo5Wa || 10 Se3 Ro1Ro5 Pi LoNa Ca ||

over this tempus in the manner of imperfect tempus of minor prolation, place four such noteshapes

If we wish to do so in the manner of imperfect tempus of major prolation, by dividing the tempus into two parts, place these noteshapes [20]

If you wish to divide two tempora of this perfect tempus into three equal parts, place these noteshapes ▫ ▫ ▫ . According to the same division of perfect tempus of major prolation, if you wish to divide it into four parts, place these noteshapes [21]

---

[20]These *figurae* will change the tempus from perfect to imperfect and so may be used to imply imperfect tempus with minor prolation as well.

[21]This example demonstrates how to write both a mode 1 (long-short) and mode 2 (short-long) rhythm.

Item si vis discantare ad modum minimarum secundum eundem actum appone tales sex figuras

vel per istum modum

Item si vis discantare ad modum temporis perfecti minoris, similiter possunt apponi tales sex || figure sicut dictum est de tempore imperfecto maioris. CS3: 122b

CAPITULUM OCTAVUM

DE TEMPORE IMPERFECTO MAIORIS PROLATIONIS

Sequitur de tempore imperfecto maioris prolationis quod si vis discantare super ipsum ad modum temporis perfecti maioris appone tales figuras

---

1 si *om.* Fa | biscantare Ca | minimarum]minoris Ro1 | eundem *om.* Ch || 2 appone has sex figuras ut hic Se3 appone has sex ut hic Fa | tales]has NaPi Ro1 | figuras ut hic LoMiWa || 3  Ch CaPiRo5Wa Na Lo || 4 per *om.* CaSe3 | istum]ipsum Na | modum ut hic Fa Se3Wa || 5 Ch Se1 Se3 Ro5 FaRo1 Pi Wa Na Ca Lo || 6 discantare] cantare PiRo1 mutare Fa *om.* Ca | temporis *om.* CaRo5Wa | perfecti *om.* Mi perfectum Ca | minoris *om.* Ca | similiter]super Ro5 || 6–7 possunt]potest Se1 posset Si || 7 poni Ro5Wa | figuras CaMiNaSe3Si | sicut]ut Ca | est *om.* Ro1 | est supra Fa | tempore]ipso Ca | perfecto minori NaPi perfecto minoris ut supra Fa | maioris et cetera Na minoris ChRo1Se1 || 8 *Cap.* 8 & 9 *permut.* Ro1 | Capitulum octavum]Sequitur de tempore imperfecto maioris Fa *om.* PiRo1 || 8–9 Capitulum ... prolationis *om.* CaLoMiNaRo5Se1Se3SiWa || 9 prolationis *om.* ChPiRo1 || 10 Sequitur]Sed Wa | Sequitur ... imperfecto maioris *om.* Na | prolationis *om.* ChFaPiRo1Ro5SiWa | vis]volueris Si || 10–94.2 Sequitur ... rubeas]Sequitur de tempore imperfecto maioris quod si vis discantare super ipsum ad modum temporis perfecti minoris prolacionis pro minimis appone sex minimas rubeas ut hic MiSe1Se3 Sequitur de tempori imperfecto maioris. Quod si vis biscantare ad modum temporis perfecti minoris prolacionis super ipsum pro minimis appone sex minimas rubeas vel vacuas Ca || 10–11 discantare]biscantare Ca || 11 ipsum]ipsas Na *om.* PiSi | ad modum temporis perfecti minoris prolationis appone tales novem minimas FaNaPiRo1 | O *in marg.* Na | perfecti *om.* Ch | maioris prolationis per minimas appone novem tales minimas Ch || 12 *8 min.* Ro5Wa ||

If you wish to discant in the manner of minimae according to the same division, place six such noteshapes  or in this manner

If you wish to discant in the manner of perfect tempus of minor prolation, six such noteshapes can similarly be placed, as was said for imperfect tempus of major prolation.[22]

CHAPTER EIGHT

ON IMPERFECT TEMPUS OF MAJOR PROLATION

Imperfect tempus of major prolation follows: if you wish to discant over this tempus in the manner of perfect tempus of major prolation, place such noteshapes [23]

---

[22] Since the tempus of this mensuration is already perfect, it is only necessary to show how to notate minor prolation. Also, as this mensuration is based on the same number of minimae as imperfect tempus with major prolation (six minimae), the same *figurae* can be used as were shown above.

[23] Void minimae are needed to change the prolation to perfect in the context of perfect tempus. The author does not show, however, how to write a mode 1 or a mode 2 rhythm in the context of perfect tempus with major prolation.

Item si vis discantare desuper ad modum temporis perfecti minoris per minimas appone sex minimas rubeas ⌜♩♩♩♩♩♩⌝

Item si vis discantare secundum eundem actum temporis perfecti minoris appone tres semibreves vacuas ut hic ◇◇◇ vel tres rubeas ut hic ⌜♦♦♦⌝

Item si vis discantare desuper ad modum temporis imperfecti minoris appone tales quatuor figuras ut hic ♩♩♩♩

CAPITULUM NONUM

DE TEMPORE PERFECTO MINORIS PROLATIONIS

Sequitur de tempore perfecto minoris prolationis quod si vis super ipsum discantare ad ‖ modum temporis perfecti maioris appone tales novem figuras ut hic ◇◇◇◇◇◇◇◇◇

CS3: 123a

Item si vis discantare desuper ad modum temporis imperfecti maioris per semibreves dividendo tempus in duas partes tunc appone duas semibreves

---

1 discantare *om.* Ro5 | desuper]super ipsum Si *om.* Lo | minoris prolationis Ro5Wa ‖ 1–2 Item si vis … sex minimas rubeas *om.* FaNaPiRo1 | per minimas *om.* Lo ‖ 2 rubeas ut hic LoRo5Wa ‖ 3 *fig. om.* LoSe1Si *min. vac.* CaSe3 *5 min. rub.* Ro5 ‖ 4 discantare]biscantare Ca | minoris]maioris Na minoris prolationis Se3 | ☉ *in marg.* Na ‖ 5 appone]appone tales figuras FaPiRo1 | appone … ut hic [*fig.*] (*sec.*)]appone tales tres figuras ◇◇◇ et cetera Na | tres (*pr.*) *om.* Se3 | semibreves … ut hic [*fig.*] (*sec.*)]semibreves vacuas uel rubeas ◇◇◇ CaSi semibreves vacuas uel tres rubeas ◇◇◇ ut patet Fa | ut hic (*pr.*) *om.* Pi | tres (*sec.*) *om.* Ro5Se1 | rubeas ut hic plenas ♦♦♦ Pi(*sine fig.*)Ro1 | ut hic (*sec.*) *om.* Se1 | *fig. om.* LoSe1 *semibr.vac.* Se3 ‖ 6 discantare]biscantare Ca *om.* MiSe3 | desuper *om.* Ca | perfecti Ro5Wa | minoris]minoris discantare Pi *om.* NaRo5Wa ‖ 7 quatuor *om.* LoSi | figuras] figuras tales Se3 *om.* Ca | ut hic]ut hic et cetera Na *om.* MiPi Ro1Ro5Si ‖ 8 ♩♩♩♩ Ch ♦♦♦♦ NaRo5Wa ♩♩♩♩ FaPi ♩♩♩♩ Ca ♦♦♦♦ Lo ‖ 9 Capitulum nonum *om.* FaMiPiRo1 ‖ 9–10 Capitulum … minoris prolationis *om.* CaLoRo5Se1Se3Wa ‖ 10 prolationis *om.* ChPiRo1 ‖ 11 Sequitur de] Et Se3 | prolationis *om.* ChRo5SiWa | vis]volueris Si | super ipsum *om.* Ca | ipsum]ipsius Pi *om.* Mi ‖ 12 discantare]biscantare Ca | perfecti maioris] imperfecti minoris prolationis Se3 | maiori Ch | novem *om.* ChMiRo1Ro5Se1 Se3Wa ‖ 12–13 tales novem minimas rubeas vel vacuas ut hic Ca ‖ 13 ut hic *om.* MiPiRo1Se1Si | *fig. 8 min.* Ro1 ‖ 14–96.1 Item si vis … semibreves punctatas ut hic]Item si vis ad partes tunc appone duas Ro1 ‖ 14 desuper] super ipsum Se1Si *om.* CaLo MiWa | temporis *om.* FaPiSe1 | perfecti Ch | minoris CaMi ‖ 14–15 per semibreves *om.* Ch ‖ 15 dividi Ca | dividendo … semibreves *om.* Se3 | tempus]tempora Ch *om.* Ca | partes equales LoSi | pone Ro5Wa ‖

If you wish to discant over it in the manner of perfect tempus of minor prolation through minimae, place six red minimae ⌐♩♩♩♩♩♩¬ [24]

If you wish to discant according to the same division of perfect tempus of minor prolation, place three hollow semibreves, as here ◇◇◇ or three red semibreves, as here ⌐◆◆◆¬ [25]

If you wish to discant over it in the manner of imperfect tempus of minor prolation, place four such noteshapes, as here ♩♩♩♩ [26]

CHAPTER NINE

ON PERFECT TEMPUS OF MINOR PROLATION

Perfect tempus of minor prolation follows: if you wish to discant over this tempus in the manner of perfect tempus of major prolation, place nine such noteshapes, as here ♩♩♩♩♩♩♩♩♩.[27]

If you wish to discant over it in the manner of imperfect tempus of major prolation through semibreves by dividing the tempus in two parts, then place

---

[24] The red notation is used to show the change in mensuration, not to imply the minimae should be imperfected.

[25] As mentioned earlier (cf. n. 16), the author prefers to use void notation to show a change of duration, although red notation is given as an alternative.

[26] As the tempus is already imperfect, it is only necessary to show how to notate the change to minor prolation.

[27] Cf. n. 23.

punctatas ut hic  item secundum eundem actum ut hic

Item si vis ad modum minimarum tunc minime debent esse rubee ut hic

5   Item si vis discantare super istud tempus ad modum temporis imperfecti minoris appone tales quatuor figuras ut hic

CAPITULUM DECIMUM

DE TEMPORE IMPERFECTO MINORIS PROLATIONIS

10   Sequitur de tempore imperfecto minoris quod si vis discantare desuper ad modum temporis imperfecti maioris, appone tales figuras ut hic

‖ Item si vis discantare desuper ad modum temporis perfecti minoris ad modum semibrevium appone tales figuras

15

---

1 ⋄·⋄· CaLo ǀ item]item si Fa ǀ secundum]si vis Ca ǀ actum per notas rubeas ut hic ♦♩♩♦ FaPiRo1(*fig. rub.*)SiWa ǀ ut hic rubeas Ro5 ‖ 2 ♩♩♩♩ Ca ♦♩♩♦ Lo ‖ 3 vis]vis discantare LoSiWa *om.* Fa ǀ minimarum]6 *min. pl.* Ro5Wa minoris ChWa minimarum secundum eundem actum LoSi ǀ tunc minime *om.* Ca ǀ minime *om.* Mi ǀ rubee vel vacue ut hic patet ♩♩♩♩♩♩♩♩ Fa ǀ ut hic demostratur Se3 ‖ 4 *fig. min. vac.* CaSe3Si *om.* LoSe1 ‖ 5 ad modum *om.* Se3 ǀ temporis *om.* FaPiRo1Se3 ǀ perfecti Ca ‖ 6 quatuor *om.* Lo ǀ ut hic *om.* CaFaMiPiRo1Si ‖ 7 ♩♩♩♩ Ch ♩♩♩♩ CaPiRo5 ♩♩♩♩ Lo ‖ 8 Capitulum decimum *om.* FaPiRo1‖ 8–9 Capitulum … minoris prolationis *om.* CaLoMiNaRo5Se1Se3SiWa ‖ 9 minori Ch ǀ prolationis *om.* ChPiRo1 ‖ 10 Sequitur de tempore imperfecto minoris *om.* Na ǀ minoris]minoris prolationis CaFaPiRo1Se1 maioris prolationis Lo ǀ quod]que Na *om.* Se1Se3 ǀ vis]volueris Si ǀ desuper]super ipsum FaMiNaRo1Si super ipsius Pi *om.* Ca ‖ 11 minoris Ro1 ǀ tales sex FaPiRo1 ǀ ut hic *om.* CaFaMiNaPiRo1Se1Si ‖ 12 *fig. min. pl.* Ch Fa ‖ 13 discantare]cantare Fa *om.* Ca ǀ desuper]super ipsum Si *om.* CaFaNaPiRo1 ǀ imperfecti maioris Se3 ǀ maioris Ro5Wa ‖ 13–14 minoris … semibrevium]minoris per semibreves dividendo ipsum tempore in tres partes Ch ǀ ad modum semibrevium]per semibreves Ca ‖ 14 semibrevibus Na ǀ tales tres FaPi ǀ figuras ut hic CaChLoSe1Se3Wa ‖ 15 ♩♩♩ Ca ⋄⋄⋄ LoNa ‖

two dotted semibreves, as here ◆· ◆·,²⁸ or again according to the same division, as here ⌈ ◆ ♩·♩· ◆ ⌝ ²⁹

If you wish to discant in the manner of minimae, then the minimae ought to be red, as here ⌈♩♩♩♩♩♩⌝

If you wish to discant over this tempus in the manner of imperfect tempus of minor prolation, place four such noteshapes, as here ♩♩♩♩

CHAPTER TEN

ON IMPERFECT TEMPUS OF MINOR PROLATION

Imperfect tempus of minor prolation follows: if you wish to discant over this tempus in the manner of imperfect tempus of major prolation, place such noteshapes as here ♩♩♩ ♩♩♩ ³⁰

If you wish to discant over it in the manner of perfect tempus of minor prolation in the manner of semibreves, place such noteshapes ♩♩♩

---

²⁸The same effect could be accomplished through the use of red notation, but again the author wishes to use something unequivocal.

²⁹This and the following example parallel the examples in chapt. 7 (pp. 89–93). The red notation is used to signal a change in mensuration, not to imply a change in duration.

³⁰As in imperfect tempus with major prolation and perfect tempus with minor prolation (cf. n. 23), the author does not demonstrate how to notate a mode 1 or mode 2 rhythm in this situation.

Item si vis discantare ad modum minimarum appone tales figuras sicut in tempore imperfecto maioris ♩♩♩ ♩♩♩

Item si vis discantare desuper ad modum temporis perfecti maioris tunc
5 accipe modum temporis perfecti minoris quia in equalitate minimarum non potest cantari, et per consequens nec scribi si recte consideres, quia non potest dividi nisi in duas partes et sic quatuor ascenderet usque ad octo et numerus sic deficeret. Sic itaque ad complementum huius operis consecutus sum ideo refero gratias deo, Amen.

10 ⟨EPILOGUS⟩

Nunc videndum est qualiter ipsas ordinabimus ad discantandum diversimode sic quatuor tempora. Et primo de tempore perfecto maioris, postea de singulis temporibus sicut inferius patebit. Ponendo rubeas de modo discan-

---

1 vis *om.* ChLo | discantare]discantare desuper Ro5 *om.* CaChLoSi | minimarum]minorum Ch minoris Ro1 | appone similiter ChLoRo5SiWa appone tales figuras ut hic Se3 | sicut *om.* Ch ‖ 1–2 minimarum ... *fig.*]minimarum ut hic patet exemplum ♩♩♩♩ et cetera Na ‖ 2 maioris ut hic ChFaLoPiSe1 maioris ut hic rubee MiRo5Wa maioris et debent esse rubee ut hic Si ‖ 3 *fig. min. rub.* Ro5 ‖ 4 discantare *om.* Ca | desuper *om.* CaFaLoNaPiRo1Se1Si | perfecti *om.* Ca | maioris]minoris Mi maioris prolationis Ca ‖ 4–5 tunc ad modum CaMiRo5Se1Se3Wa ‖ 5 accipe]accipit Ch *om.* CaMiSe1Se3 | modum ... minoris]ad modum temporis predicti Wa | minoris]maioris Se1 | quia]que NaSe3 | equalitate]equaliter Mi qualitate Ca ‖ 6 cantari]cantare Ch Lo *om.* Ca | per *om.* Se3 | per consequens]ergo Se1 | consequens nec]quam Lo | nec]non CaMiNaPiRo1Se1Se3 *om.* LoSi | si]sed Na | consideras ChLo MiSe1Se3SiWa consideret Ro1 | quia]que Se3 | non *om.* Ca ‖ 7 nisi *om.* CaNa | et sic *om.* Ca | sic]si ChLoMiNaPiRo1Se1Wa *om.* Se3 | ascenderint Ch ascendetur FaPi ascenderent LoRo5Si Wa ascendentur Na ascenderit Se3 | ad *om.* ChLoSi ‖ 8 numerus]numeris Ca numeraveritis Mi nunc Ro5Wa unus Lo | sic *om.* Si | deficeretis Lo deficet Pi deficerent Ro5Wa deficeret et cetera Si | Sicque CaSi | itaque]ipsum que Se3 | completionem Lo | huius]unius Se3 | operis]temporis Ch | assecutus Ro1 secutus Se1 ‖ 8–9 Sic ... Amen *om.* Fa ‖ 9 sum]fui Se3 *om.* Ca | ideo]deo Pi *om.* Mi | refero semper Ca | deo]Christo Se1 Domino Iehsu Christo Se3 | Amen *om.* MiNaPiRo1 Ro5Si ‖ 10 *scripsi* ‖ 11–102 *om.* CaChSe3 ‖ 11 *ante* Nunc videndum] Superius dictum est de augmentatione atque diminutione figurarum LoRo5Wa Qualiter ordinatur ad discantandum Si | dicendum MiRo5Wa | qualiter] quomodo Ro1 | ordinabis LoRo5SiWa | quod vis cantandum Ro5 | discantandum sic Na ‖ 11–12 diversimodi Si diversi Lo ‖ 12 sic]super Ro5SiWa secundum Fa de super Lo | primo]postea Lo | tempori Wa | perfecto *om.* FaLo ‖ 13 singulis]similiter Lo | sicut]ut Mi | patebunt Lo patet Si patebit et cetera PiRo1Se1 | Ponendo *om.* Mi | Ponendo rubeas *om.* LoRo5SiWa | rubee Mi ‖ 13–100.1 discantati Pi ‖

If you wish to discant in the manner of minimae, place such noteshapes as in imperfect tempus of major prolation ♩♩♩♩♩♩

If you wish to discant over it in the manner of perfect tempus of major prolation, then take the manner of perfect tempus of minor prolation because in the equality of minimae it cannot be sung or, consequently, written if you will consider correctly, because a minima cannot be divided except into two parts,[31] and thus four will increase to eight and the number will thus be deficient. As I have come to the completion of this work, I therefore give thanks to God, Amen.

EPILOGUE[32]

Now must be seen how we will order these same noteshapes for discanting in various ways as the four tempora. First, on perfect tempus of major prolation, afterwards by the individual tempora, as will be shown below. By placing red noteshapes for the manner of discanting, which in the vulgar

---

[31]That is, four minimae can only be divided into eight semiminimae and so are one note short of the nine needed to imply perfect tempus with major prolation.

[32]Three sources (Lo, Si, Se1) contain extended notation examples at the close of this final section. The examples from Se1 are particularly extensive and accurate and will be given in the Appendix.

100

tandi qui dicitur secundum illos de francia vulgariter trayn vel traynour est fortior modus quam sincopare. In primo de tempore perfecto maioris ponuntur ‖ pro duobus temporibus novem semibreves rubee vel vacue ut hic

CS?
124

      Tenor   Discantus

5   Item de tempore perfecto minoris

      Tenor   Discantus

‖ Item de tempore imperfecto maioris

CS:
124

      Tenor   Discantus

---

1 qui]quod FaRo5 quia NaSe1 | dicitur]dicti Wa *om.* Si | illos de francia] gallicos LoRo5SiWa | vulgariter]vulgare Lo *om.* Si | trayn vel traynour] traneum vel trahyn et Ro5Wa trameum vel tram (?) et Si traim (?) vel trainour Na tranon vel tranbue et Mi carmen vel carmen et Lo ‖ 2 fortior]formalior Ro5 | quam]qua tum Mi | primo]principio Se1 post Lo | maiorum Fa | ☉ *in marg.* Na ‖ 2–3 ponitur MiNa ‖ 3 semibreves vacue ut hic rubee Pi | rubee vel *om.* LoMiRo1Se1SiWa | ut hic apparet inferius per exemplum NaRo1 | ut hic ↓↓↓↓↓↓↓↓ Lo ‖ 4 *ante fig.* trainer vel traineir MiSe1 de tempori perfecto maiori Wa |  Wa *semibr. sep.* LoNaRo5Se1SiWa *fig. om.* Ro1 ‖ 5 Item de tempore perfecto minoris]Discantus de tempore perfecto minoris Wa Rubet discantus de tempore perfecto minoris Mi *om.* NaRo1Se1 | tempore *om.* Si | imperfecto Wa | minoris sequitur ut hic FaPi ‖ 6 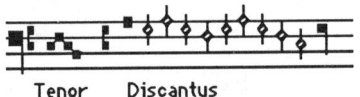 FaPi Na Wa *om.* Mi ‖ 7 Item de tempore imperfecto maioris]Discantus de tempore imperfecto maioris Wa Discantans de tempore imperfecto maioris Mi *om.* NaRo1Se1 | tempore *om.* Si | maioris sequitur ut hic FaPi ‖ 8 LoNaSe1Si FaPi Wa ‖

tongue is called by those of France *trayn* or *traynour*,[33] there is a more energetic manner than in syncopation. First, on perfect tempus of major prolation, nine red or hollow semibreves are placed for two tempora, as here

On perfect tempus of minor prolation

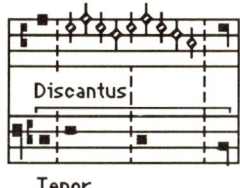

On imperfect tempus of major prolation

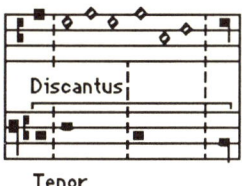

---

[33]For a discussion of *traynour*, see the Introduction, pp. 20–23.

Item de tempore imperfecto minoris

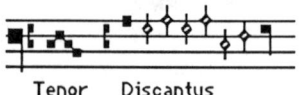

Tenor   Discantus

Item de semibrevibus perfectis

Tenor   Discantus

---

1 Item de tempore imperfecto minoris]Discantus de tempore imperfecto minoris Wa Discantans de tempore imperfecto minoris Mi Item sequitur de tempore imperfecto ut hic FaPi *om.* NaRo1Se1 | tempore *om.* Si | et sic est finis totius libri Fa ‖ 2 [music] Pi [music] FaLo [music] Wa ‖ 3 Item de semibrevibus perfectis]Discantus de semibrevibus perfectis Wa Discantans de semibrevibus perfectis Mi *om.* FaNaPiRo1Se1 ‖ 4 [music] Lo NaSi [music] Wa ‖

On imperfect tempus of minor prolation

Discantus

Tenor

On perfect semibreves

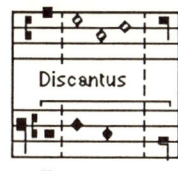

Discantus

Tenor

APPENDIX

Three sources (Lo, Si, Se1) contain an extended set of notation examples following the *Tractatus figurarum*. The examples in Lo and Si are brief and nearly illegible. The examples in Se1, however, are extensive and carefully drawn, showing the copyist understood the material with which he was working. He has organized them into four groups, each preceded by a mensuration sign. Each group begins with the standard example of *traynour* given in most sources of the *Tractatus figurarum* and then expands to more creative rhythmic possibilities. These examples go beyond the *Tractatus* in that they are no longer necessarily concerned with the rhythmic imitation of another mensuration, but rather with what is possible in a more abstract sense, given the rhythmic duration of the *figurae*. It is clear from the accuracy and creativity of these examples that whoever wrote them had a firm enough grasp of the *Tractatus*'s notational principles to be able to build upon them. What follow, then, are the examples from the Seville manuscript reproduced in score format and accompanied by brief annotations.

Perfect tempus with major prolation

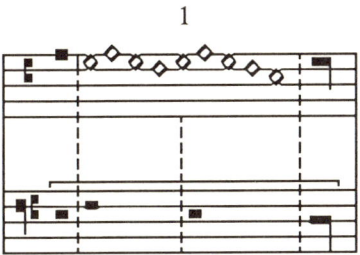

1

Above is the first example of *traynour* mentioned in the Epilogue. It is written here without ligatures in the upper voice.

2

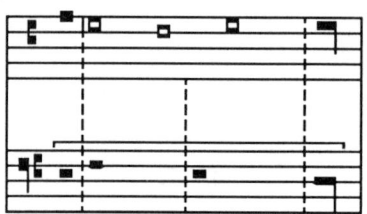

According to chapter 6 (82.10–11), three hollow breves are to be used to replace two tempora of perfect tempus with major prolation.

3

Here is an example of the *figurae* used to perform in the manner of imperfect tempus while in perfect tempus with major prolation.

4

These *figurae* are equivalent to those in 1 and produce the identical rhythm.

5

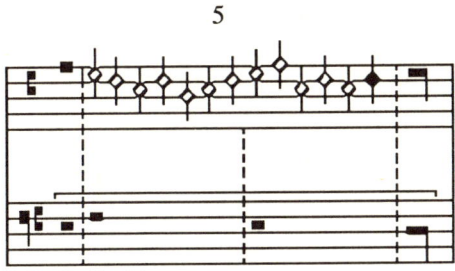

Each group of three hollow *dragmae* is equivalent to four minimae, and so the four groups present are equivalent to sixteen minimae. When their value is added to that of the one solid *dragma*, the requisite eighteen minimae are accounted for.

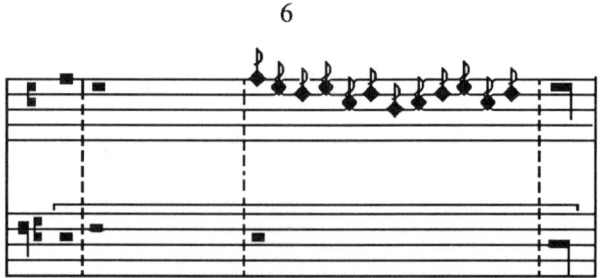

Four imperfect minimae are equivalent to three minimae, and so these twelve are equivalent to nine minimae. This example appears to be mimicking the Italian *divisio*, *duodenaria*.

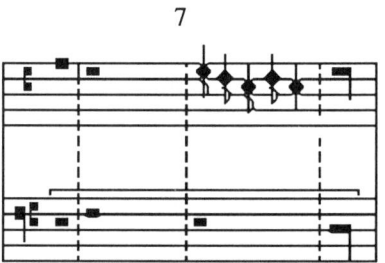

The four *figurae* that are a combination of a minima and an imperfect minima are equivalent to seven minimae and so together with the *dragma* are equivalent to nine minimae.

8

Four of the above *figurae* are equivalent to nine minimae and are used to perform in the manner of imperfect tempus with minor prolation while in perfect tempus with major prolation.

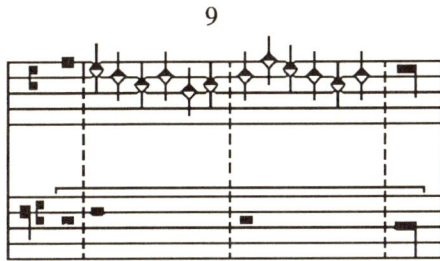

9

Each of the above *figurae* should be the combination of a minima and a semiminima, and so the descending stem should also have a flag. They are to be used in this mensuration to perform in the manner of perfect tempus with minor prolation or imperfect tempus with major prolation.

10

[musical notation]

Three hollow minimae are equivalent to two solid, and so the above group of twelve is equivalent to eight minimae. When these are added to the single solid minima, the required nine minimae are accounted for.

11

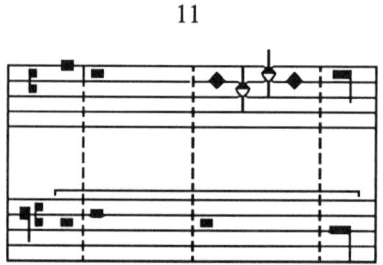

As in 9, the two *figurae* with descending tails should also have flags on them.

12

This is the only example of the twenty that makes no sense. If, however, each of the first four *figurae* over the F in the tenor were actually the combination of a minima and an imperfect minima, then they (being equivalent to seven minimae)—when added to the single *dragma*—would complete the required nine minimae needed for one brevis in this mensuration.

Imperfect tempus with major prolation

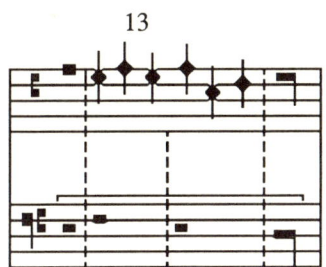

13

This is the example of *traynour* given in the *Tractatus figurarum* for this mensuration. In this case, *dragmae* have been substituted for hollow semibreves.

14

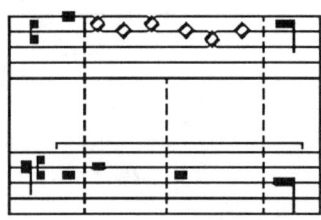

This example is rhythmically equivalent to the above.

15

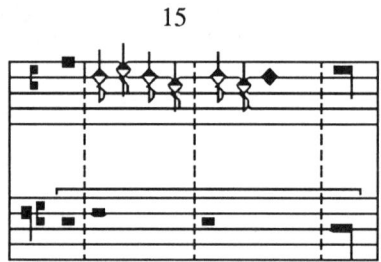

These *figurae* are used in this mensuration to perform in the manner of imperfect tempus with minor prolation.

Perfect tempus with minor prolation

16

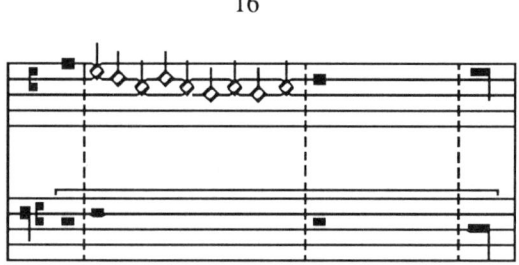

This example allows one to perform in the manner of perfect tempus with major prolation.

17

This example allows one to perform in the manner of imperfect tempus.

18

This example allows one to perform in the manner of imperfect tempus with minor prolation.

Imperfect tempus with minor prolation

19

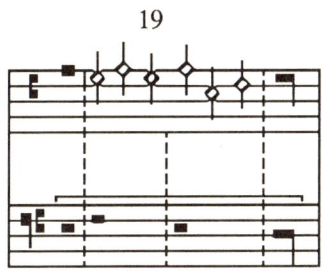

This is the example of *traynour* prescribed by the *Tractatus* for this mensuration.

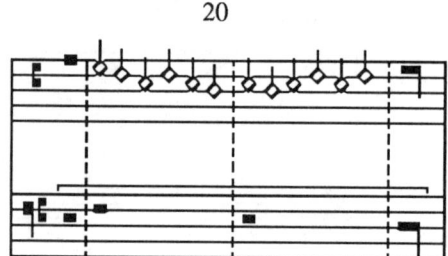

20

This final example allows one to perform in the manner of perfect tempus with minor prolation or imperfect tempus with major prolation.

INDEX VERBORUM

abhorrere, *v.* Tribum que non abhorruit
abstrahere, 84.7
accipere, 72.11; 74.1, 6; 78.1; 98.5
actus, 90.8; 92.1; 94.4; 96.1
additio, 74.5
adiungi, 82.5–6; 84.1; 86.8
adiutorium, 72.3, 74.7–8
alius, 66.8; 78.3; 82.1, 6, 7; 84.11
alter, 66.4; 72.8
ambo, 80.12; 82.1
amittere, 76.4, 7, 9, 12; 88.6
antecessor, 68.4
antiquus, 66.6
apponere, 90.2, 5, 8, 9; 92.2, 11; 94.2, 5, 7, 12, 15; 96.6, 11, 14; 98.1; apponi, 92.7
Apta caro, 68.2
ars, 68.1
ascendere, 82.1; 98.7
augmentari, 74.5
augmentatio, 74.6, 8; 80.2, 3, 4; 82.3, 6, 9; 88.12
brevis, 68.9; 70.3; 74.5, 10; 76.8; 78.6; 80.5, 7, 10, 12; 82.10
cantari, 98.6
cantor, 80.6
caro, *v.* Apta caro
cauda, 86.5
caudari, 74.6; 84.4; 86.5; 88.2
clare, 70.10; 72.2
clarus, 74.4, 7
cognosci, 80.9
communis, 84.5
complementum, 98.8
computare, 84.8; 86.9
confici, 68.4

consequens, 98.6
consequi, 98.8–9
considerare, 68.1; 72.9; 80.3; 82.5; 98.6
cor, 66.5
corpus, 78.3; 88.1
curare, 72.2
dare, 80.8; 82.6
debere, 70.9; 76.14; 96.3
declarare, 76.15
deficere, 98.8
descendere, 80.4, 12
desiderare, 66.5
deus, 72.3; 74.7; 98.9
dexter, 74.6
dicere, 72.3; 80.7, 8; 88.6; dici, 76.5; 88.12; 92.7; 100.1
dictus, 78.3
dilatio, 80.6
dimidietas, 78.2
diminutio, 72.6, 11; 74.1–2, 4, 8; 78.1; 80.4–5; 82.3, 9; 88.12
discantare, 70.9; 90.1; 92.1, 6, 10–11; 94.1, 4, 6, 12, 14; 96.5, 10, 13; 98.1, 4, 11, 13–100.1; discantari, 66.3; 72.7; 82.6–7
discantus, 100.4, 6, 8; 102.2, 4
diversimode, 66.3; 72.7; 82.6; 86.1; 98.11–12
dividere, 78.7, 8; 82.12; 90.4, 7, 9; 94.15; dividi, 78.3; 98.7
docere, 70.8
dominus, 66.4
dubium, 72.10; 74.7
duo, 74.3; 76.7, 9, 12; 78.4 (bis), 7, 8, 9; 82.4, 11, 12; 84.1, 5; 88.7; 90.4, 7; 94.15 (bis); 98.7; 100.3
duplex longa, 68.9; 70.3; 74.9; 76.3; 80.5
effectus, 72.3; 84.12, 13
effici, 80.11
epilogus, 98.10
equalis, 82.12; 90.8
equalitas, 98.5
evacuare, 78.7, 86.3; evacuari, 72.10; 76.4, 6–7, 8–9, 12, 14; 84.7; 88.6
evacuatio, 72.10–11; 74.9; 76.2
evasio, 80.6
facere, 78.9; 80.7–8; 88.7

figura, 66.1, 3; 68.7, 8; 70.5; 72.6, 7; 76.2; 78.2–3, 3; 80.2, 3, 10; 82.6, 9; 84.1, 11; 86.1, 2, 5; 88.5, 10, 12; 90.2, 5, 8, 9; 92.2, 7, 11; 94.7, 12; 96.6, 11, 14; 98.1
figurari, 86.1
fortior, 100.2
francia, 100.1
gradatim, 80.4
gratia, 72.11; 74.5; 80.10; 98.9
gratiose, 66.5
grossus, 66.7
habere, 66.6; 68.2–3; 78.2; 84.12, 13, 14; 86.2
homo, 86.2
imperfectio, 72.11; 74.2
imperfectus, 68.4; 70.4; 74.5; 84.3, 5, 11; *v.* tempus imperfectum maioris prolationis, tempus imperfectum minoris prolationis
imperfici, 74.4
incipere, 66.3
inconveniens, 72.1
inferior, 80.12
instruere, 70.5
intellectus, 66.6
intelligens, 68.3; 72.3–4; 74.3
intendere, 74.7
invenire, 84.7; inveniri, 74.1
licere, 66.5; 70.5; 80.8; liceri, 86.2–3
ligari, 80.10
longa, 68.9; 70.3; 74.9; 76.6; 80.5, 10; *v.* duplex longa
magis, 68.1
magister, 66.6, 7; 68.3, 7, 8; 70.5; 80.8
maior, 68.3; 84.12; *v.* tempus imperfectum maioris prolationis, tempus perfectum maioris prolationis
manifestus, 68.8–9
mensura, 70.6
meritum, 76.14
minima, 68.10; 70.4; 74.3, 10; 76.11, 12, 14; 78.5, 6, 8, 9; 80.9; 82.2, 5, 14; 84.2, 4, 5, 8, 10, 11, 12, 13; 86.6, 9; 88.1, 2, 5, 6, 7; 92.1; 94.2 (bis); 96.2 (bis); 98.1, 5
minor, 78.3, 4, 5; 82.5; 84.13; *v.* tempus imperfectum minoris prolationis, tempus perfectum minoris prolationis
modus, 66.7, 8; 68.1; 74.5; 76.3; 82.7; 90.1, 4; 92.1, 4, 6, 11; 94.1, 6, 12, 14; 96. 3, 5, 11, 13, 14; 98.1, 4, 5, 13; 100.2

motetus, 66.7
multum, 72.1; 74.7
musica, 66.5; 80.8
musicalis, 66.6
necesse, 80.4
nichil, 78.2; 80.8
novem, 84.2; 86.9; 94.12; 100.3
nullus, 78.2
numerare, 78.3
numerus, 98.8
octo, 98.7
omnis, 68.8; 72.9
opera, 98.8
oportere, 80.9
ordinare, 68.2; 72.2; 88.10, 13; 98.11; ordinari, 72.7
ordo, 66.4; 72.8
ostendere, 72.2, 7; 74.9; 88.13; ostendi, 74.8
pars, 74.2, 6; 76.4, 7, 9, 12, 14; 78. 4, 7, 8 (bis); 80.12 (bis); 82.10, 12; 84.7; 88.6; 90.5, 7, 9; 94.15; 98.7
parvulus, 72.2
patere, 66.7; 68.2; 70.10–72.1, 4; 82.4; 98.13
pausa, 70.3
pausatio, 70.2
perdere, 74.2; 76.14; 82.10
perfectio, 78.1
perfectus, 70.4; 72.10; 74.1, 4; 76.3, 6, 8, 11; 82.14; 102.3; *v.* tempus perfectum maioris prolationis, tempus perfectum minoris prolationis
perficere, 84.1; perfici, 84.3
perlustrare, 66.5
plenitudo, 72.10
plenus, 72.9; 82.2; 84.13
plus, 80.6
ponere, 98.13; poni, 82.10; 84.12; 86.1; 100.2–3
posse, 72.1, 2; 78.4; 82.5, 6, 11; 86.1, 2; 92.6–7; 98.6, 7
primus, 66.6; 68.1, 3
principalis, 70.6
procedere, 74.8
producere, 72.3
prolatio, 78.4; 82.5; *v.* tempus imperfectum maioris prolationis, tempus imperfectum minoris prolationis, tempus perfectum maioris prolationis, tempus perfectum minoris prolationis

prologus, 66.2
pronuntiari, 72.1
proprietas, 76.3, 6, 8, 11; 80.11 (bis); 82.3; 84.14
punctari, 82.14; 96.1
punctus, 78.1, 5, 7; 84.3; 86.8
qualitas, 80.10
quatuor, 70.6; 76.5; 82.14; 84.7–8, 10, 12; 86.5–6, 9; 90.2, 9; 94.7; 96.6; 98.7, 12
ratio, 72.9
recte, 82.5; 84.8; 86.9; 98.6
referre, 98.9
reformari, 68.5
relinquere, 68.1, 3; relinqui, 68.4, 8
reperiri, 70.4
requiescere, 80.6
res, 72.9; 74.4, 5
retorqueri, 86.5; 88.2
rubeus, 86.1, 2; 94.2, 5; 96.3; 98.13; 100.3
scientia, 66.5
scribere, 86.2; scribi, 70.5; 72.2; 98.6
semibrevis, 68.9; 70.3; 72.11–74.1, 9, 10; 76.4, 8, 9, 11; 78.6; 82.1, 14; 84.3, 4–5; 94.5, 15 (bis); 96.14; 100.3; 102.3
semiminima, 78.4, 8; 80.7; 82.4; 84.1, 13, 14; 86.8–9; 88.2–3, 5
semiplenus, 88.1
semivacuus, 88.1
septem, 86.6
sequi, 66.4; 72.8; 92.10; 94.11; 96.10
sex, 76.3; 92.2, 7; 94.2
signum, 80.9; 82.2; 84.14
similis, 74.4
similiter, 76.14; 92.6
sincopare, 100.2
singulariter, 70.10
singulus, 70.10; 98.13
sinister, 80.12; 82.1
studium, 68.4
subtilior, 66.8–68.1
subtilitas, 68.3
subtiliter, 68.1–2
successor, 68.5
superior, 82.1

suscipere, 82.3
tempus, 66.4; 70.10; 72.8; 76.3, 5, 6, 7; 82.11–12; 88.10, 13; 90.4, 7; 94.15; 96.5; 98.12, 13; 100.3; tempus imperfectum maioris prolationis, 86.3–4; 92.9, 10, tempus imperfectum maioris [prolationis], 90.4; 92.7; 94.14; 96.11; 98.2; 100.7, tempus imperfectum [maioris prolationis], 70.7; tempus imperfectum minoris prolationis, 96.9, tempus imperfectum minoris [prolationis], 70.9; 90.2; 94.6; 96.5–6, 10; 102.1, tempus imperfectum [minoris prolationis], 70.8; tempus perfectum maioris prolationis, 70.6–7; 88.11, 13–90.1, tempus perfectum maioris [prolationis], 82.11; 90.9; 92.11; 94.12; 98.4, 12; 100.2, tempus perfectum [maioris prolationis], 90.7; tempus perfectum minoris prolationis, 70.7–8, 86.4; 94.10, 11, tempus perfectum minoris [prolationis], 92.6; 94.1, 4; 96.13; 98.5; 100.5, [tempus] perfectum minoris [prolationis], 70.9
tenere, 80.9
tenor, 66.4; 72.8 (bis); 82.7; 100.4, 6, 8; 102.2, 4
tertius, 74.2; 76.4, 7, 9, 12, 14; 78.2; 82.10; 84.7; 88.6
tractatus, 66.1, 3; 72.2
tradi, 68.7
trayn, 100.1
traynour, 100.1
tres, 74.3; 76.6, 8, 11; 84.10, 12; 88.7; 90.7; 94.5 (bis)
Tribum que non abhorruit, 66.8
unus, 78.8; 82.4; 88.1
vacuus, 74.1; 78.1; 82.2; 86.8; 94.5; 100.3
valere, 74.3 (bis); 76.3, 5, 6, 7, 8, 9, 11, 12; 78.5, 6, 7; 82.4, 14; 84.1, 4, 10; 86.6, 8, 9; 88.2
valor, 76.15; 78.5
velle, 80.7, 11; 90.1, 7, 9; 92.1, 6, 10; 94.1, 4, 6, 11, 14; 96.3, 5, 10, 13; 98.1, 4
venire, 68.2
verbum, 72.11; 74.5; 80.10
via, 72.9; 74.9
videri, 80.3; 98.11
virtus, 74.2; 76.4, 7, 9, 12, 15; 82.10; 88.6
vocari, 82.4; 84.11
vulgariter, 100.1

INDEX NOMINUM ET RERUM

additae, 18, 85n.15
Andrea, Phillipoctus, 4, 33
Apta caro, 10, 11, 68–69
Aquinas, Thomas, 1
Ars nova, 2; *see also* Vitry
Ars subtilior, 1, 13, 20
Beldomandi, Prosdocimo de': *Expositiones tractatus pratice cantus mensurabilis magistri Johannis de Muris* of, 14–15; discussion of semiminima in, 15n.47
Berkeley manuscript, 17; function of descending tail in, 17n.51, 85n.14; reference to *additae* in, 18n.52; reference to *fusa* in, 17n.49
Boen, Johannes: *Ars musicae* of, hollow dot in, 13n.42; omission of semiminima in, 9
Bonadies, Frater, 4, 9, 36
Caserta, Philippus de: as author of *Tractatus figurarum*, 3–5, 9, 61; *En remirant* of, 5
Codex Vindobonensis, 59; *see also* Newberry Library manuscript
composite noteshapes, 16, 24, 85n.13–14, 87n.17, 89n.18
De modo componendi: *see* Murino
Durham manuscript, 11
Egidius de Murino: *see* Murino
equal brevis, 24
figura: description in *Tractatus figurarum*, 15–20
Frater Bonadies: *see* Bonadies
fusa, 17n.49, 85n.14, 89n.18
hollow dot, 13–14, 18, 78–79, 86–87
imperfect minimae, 17–18, 18, 84–85, 87n.17, 106, 111
intentio secunda, 1
Ivrea manuscript, 11
Jacques de Liège: *see* Liège
Johannes Boen: *see* Boen
Johannes de Muris: *see* Muris

Liège, Jacques de, 3, 8
minima: mensurability of, 19
minor valor, 14, 19, 23, 78–79
Montpellier codex, 10
Murino, Egidius de: as author of *Tractatus figurarum*, 3, 5–9, 38–39, 47, 60; *De modo componendi* of, 6–7n.19, linking of, to *Tractatus figurarum*, 3, 6–7, 46n.88, 47, 60
Muris, Johannes de: *Ars contrapuncti* of, 61; *Libellus* of, 61; *Notitia artis musicae* of, 1, 69n.5, definition of *sincopa* in, 21n.60
Newberry Library manuscript: colophon to, 33n.68; description of, 31–33; *see also* Codex Vindobonensis
Pareja, Ramos de: *Musica pratica* of, 5–6; quotes from *Tractatus figurarum* in, 6n.16
Pepusch, Johann Christoph, 38, 59
Phillipoctus Andrea: *see* Andrea
Philippe de Vitry: *see* Vitry
Philippus de Caserta: *see* Caserta
Prosdocimo de' Beldomandi: *see* Beldomandi
Quatuor principalia musicae, 20
Ramos de Pareja: *see* Pareja
Red notation, 12, 18, 24, 86–87, 95n.24–25, 97n.28–29; Philippe de Vitry on use of, 12n.40, 71n.6
semiminima: importance placed on in *Tractatus figurarum*, 7–8; in French theory, 8–9; justification for use in *Tractatus figurarum*, 14, 80–83
Senleches, 2; *Harpe de Melodie* of, 33
sincopa, 20–21; definition of, by Johannes de Muris, 21n.60
subtilitas, 6
Tractatus figurarum: authorship of, 3–9; commentary on, 4, 52; epilogue to, 20–23; evolution of notation in, 9–11; stemma of, 59–64; theory of, 11–15
tractatus verborum, 21
traynour, 16, 20–21, 39, 46, 52, 54, 100–101, 105; examples of, in *Tractatus figurarum*, 22–23, 100–103; extended examples of: *see* Appendix
Trémoïlle manuscript, 11
Tribum que non abhorruit, see Vitry
Vitry, Philippe de: *Ars nova* of, 3, 8, 8n.26, 10, on immensurability of minima, 19n.53; *Tribum que non abhorruit* of, 10, 11, 66–67